Accelerating Health Reforms through Collective Action

A WORLD BANK STUDY

Accelerating Health Reforms through Collective Action

Experiences from East Africa

Yvonne Nkrumah and Julia Mensah, Editors

WORLD BANK GROUP

Contents

Boxes

Figures

Table

Acknowledgments

As part of the drive to increase resource efficiency and improve health outcomes through better governance in pharmaceutical procurement and supply chain management (PSM), the World Bank Institute's Health Systems Practice (WBIHS) and the Open Governance Practice (WBIOG) initiated a multiyear capacity-building initiative, which will bring multiple stakeholders involved in the medicines supply chain process to forge consensus on governance challenges, identify areas for action and improvement, initiate peer-to-peer learning and facilitate the implementation of measures to improve transparency and accountability in PSM. Since January 2010, a group of dedicated professionals and civil society actors in Kenya, Tanzania and Uganda has worked together with colleagues from the World Bank Group to carry out actions to facilitate needed reforms through capacity development to enhance policy action. We gratefully acknowledge their continuing efforts.

With the strategic guidance of Maria-Luisa Escobar (Practice Manager, WBIHS) and Robert Hunja (Practice Manager, WBIOG), the Initiative to Improve PSM Governance was task managed by Yvonne Nkrumah (Senior Operations Officer) and Julia Mensah (Extended Term Consultant). The concept note for the program received useful comments and invaluable input from Dominic Haazen, Keith Hansen, Akiko Maeda, Andre Medici, Michael Mills, Fernando Montenegro, Peter Okwero, Sangeeta Raja, Michael Reich, Andreas Seiter and Hiba Tahboub. As this initiative has progressed, we have received advice and encouragement from several colleagues from the Bank: Kobina Aidoo, Kidus Fisaha Asfaw, Joy de Beyer, Marylou Bradley, Lyudmila Bujoreanu, Ed Campos, Leonardo Cubillos-Turriago, Adarsh A. Desai, Kathrin Frauscher, Jenny Gold, Xiaohui Hou, Wacuka W. Ikua, Roberto Iunes, Sheila Jagannathan, Emmanuel Malangalila, Nicolas Meyer, Paul Mutebi, Barbara Ndamira, Lydia Ndebele, Antonio Panigua-Martin, G.N.V. Ramana, Marcela Rozo, Arathi Sundaravadana, Jeff Thindwa, Caby Verzosa, and Jourdan Woo.

The authors of the country-specific chapters were Debra Gichio, Abel Nyakiongora, and Teresa Omondi for Kenya; Jacqueline Idusso, Joseph Mhando, and Eva Ombaka for Tanzania; and Jacqueline Idusso, Emmanuel Higenyi, and Robinah Kaitiritimba for Uganda. The Uganda chapter also benefitted from significant contributions from Martin Oteba, Assistant Commissioner-Pharmacy

Division/MoH, and Denis Kibira, Deputy Executive Director, HEPS Uganda. They have carefully distilled their deep involvement and rich experience in their respective multistakeholder coalitions to provide the knowledge captured in this book. We salute their partnership and commitment in this initiative to achieve sustainable reforms, and ongoing documentation of activities, including challenges and lessons learned.

Many behind-the-scenes activities take place between producing a manuscript and seeing a printed book. We would therefore like to thank the following colleagues. Stephanie Debere's editorial skills helped to bring out the gems in the chapters. Richard Crabbe provided editorial and communications advice and started off the authors with a presentation on "How to write to be understood". Will Kemp created and designed the layout from our rudimentary descriptions, and Adam Broadfoot ensured that we got this printed right on time.

It has been a rewarding experience to have participated in and coordinated this effort and to have worked with such committed colleagues within and outside the Bank.

About the Contributors

Debra Gichio serves as coordinator of the Governance and Policy program at Transparency International Kenya, and has over eight years' working experience in governance, with emphasis on litigation, human rights, anticorruption, and institutional reforms. She is an advocate of the High Court of Kenya, and has previously worked with the Kenya National Human Rights Commission and the Independent Medical Legal Unit, among others. In her current capacity at Transparency International Kenya, she coordinates implementation of the legislative, political accountability, institutional strengthening, climate governance, and procurement programs. Debra also currently convenes the multistakeholder coalition, Forum for Transparency and Accountability in Pharmaceutical Procurement (FoTAPP), the Contract Monitoring Network- Kenya (CMNK), and the East African Good Governance and Human Rights Platform. She holds a Bachelor of Law from the University of Nairobi and a postgraduate diploma in law and practice.

Emmanuel Higenyi is head of capacity building at the Joint Medical Store (JMS), Uganda, with responsibility for training hospital and program managers in all aspects of medicines management or drug supply: regulation, quality assurance, financing, selection, quantification, procurement, inventory control, storage, distribution, utilization, and disposal. He has nearly 10 years' experience with pharmaceutical supply chain management in different settings and at different levels: service provision, distribution, technical assistance, and research. He also has specialized training in drug supply, research, quality management systems, data analysis, and good manufacturing practice (GMP) audit. Higenyi has conducted extensive research with experience in study designs, data management, analysis, and interpretation, with particular focus on health systems research in pharmaceutical supply chains in the public and private sectors. Higenyi holds a bachelor's degree in pharmacy from Makerere University and a master's degree in public health from the International Health Sciences University, both in Uganda. In addition, he holds postgraduate diplomas in project management, statistics, business, and legal studies.

Jacqueline Idusso is a key account manager for Merck Sharp and Dohme, Uganda. In this role, she is a member of the Family Planning Working Group, Maternal and Child Health cluster, and the Technical Working Group on Medicines Procurement and Management organized at the Ministry of Health. With the creation of Merck's Institutional Business (Africa), her responsibilities have increased progressively to include Human Papillomavirus (HPV) vaccination, HIV, Merck for Mothers, and support to the Mectizan Donation Program. Using her experience in network development, she worked closely with the Ministry of Health and the HPV Technical Advisory Group to successfully launch HPV vaccination following the signing of a memorandum of understanding between Merck Sharp and Dohme and the Government of Uganda. Prior to joining Merck, she served as the National Coordinator of the Medicines Transparency Alliance—the local multistakeholder coalition in Uganda. She has also served in various capacities in Population Services International (PSI), a leading international non-governmental organization. Idusso is a registered pharmacist with experience in supply chain management and social marketing.

Robinah Kaitiritimba is the executive director for the Uganda National Health Consumers' Organization (UNHCO) and a patient champion for the WHO Patient Safety Programme. She also leads a coalition of patients' organizations, Voices for Health Rights, which is currently implementing a maternal health project funded by the Swedish International Development Cooperation Agency (SIDA). As the lead coordinator for civil society organizations (CSOs), she has mobilized over 30 CSOs to rally support for Uganda's Maternal Health Petition No. 16 and budget advocacy for the health sector. Kaitiritimba is a member of the Health Policy Advisory Committee, Uganda Health Marketing Group (UHMG), National Health Insurance Task Force, and Public Private Partnership in Health. She serves on the Makerere University School of Public Health Institutional Review Board and on the National Biosafety Committee for the Uganda National Council for Science and Technology. She has made presentations and carried out research on topics including human rights and quality of health. One of her major achievements has been empowering people to improve health care user participation and overall health outcomes for vulnerable communities, and the development of the Patients' Charter for Uganda. She holds a master's degree in public administration and management and a Bachelor of Arts (sociology and political science). She has trained in health and human rights, NGO management, integrating gender and health for poverty reduction, and policy advocacy.

Julia Mensah is a public policy analyst with a broad background in public sector management, economic development, and coalition building. Currently a consultant at the World Bank Institute (WBI), she specializes in developing the capacity of public sector, private sector, and civil society actors to work collaboratively in accelerating policy reforms . She has supported multistakeholder coalitions in East Africa to implement catalytic initiatives focused on improving transparency, accountability, and citizen participation in health care service delivery. Prior to joining the World Bank in 2010, she worked at the U.S. Project on National Security Reform. Between 2005 and 2008, she was a research associate at the National Academy of Public Administration, where she helped design innovative approaches to enable agencies to transition to new visions and next-generation systems. She holds a master's degree in public policy from Harvard University.

Joseph Mhando is a senior lecturer and dean of the School of Pharmacy at the St. John's University of Tanzania, which is also the national convener of the local multistakeholder coalition. He is a registered pharmacist, with extensive experience in pharmaceutical procurement and supply chain management, having held senior leadership positions in parastatal and private pharmaceutical manufacturing and distribution organizations in Tanzania. He has been involved with the multistakeholder coalition, MSG-Pharma, since its creation in 2011, and is currently its chairman.

Yvonne Nkrumah is a senior operations officer at the World Bank Institute. Since joining the Bank in 2007, she has identified new areas for program development in governance and pharmaceutical procurement, provided technical assistance and coaching to Bank clients on strengthening demand-side engagement and result-based methodologies, and designed and delivered capacity building programs for the health sector. Prior to joining WBI, she served in various positions in Ghana's public service, where she provided legal and policy advice on health, procurement, food and drugs regulation, intellectual property rights, and access to medicines. She holds an undergraduate law degree, is a barrister-at-law, and has a master's degree in international affairs. Her main professional interests are access to medicines and collective action for reforms. She has co-authored a book, *Improving Access to HIV/AIDS Medicines in Africa*, and her article, "TRIPS Compliance and Public Health: Opportunities & Obstacles for Africa", was published in the International Journal of Biotechnology.

Abel Nyakiongora is a medical doctor with a master's degree in public health (management of health systems and services). He has also received extensive training in strategic leadership and project management at the Kenya School of Government. Nyakiongora has wide-ranging experience in health care service provision and management. He currently works as an assistant director of medical services in the Directorate of Policy, Planning and Healthcare Financing at Kenya's Ministry of Health, where he is engaged in policy development and strategic planning for health. Nyakiongora is also the focal person for social accountability in the Ministry of Health and in that capacity, has been an active member of the FoTAPP multistakeholder coalition, and of CMNK, a grouping of civil society, development partners, private sector, government, and semi-autonomous government agencies. Recently Nyakiongora has been instrumental in developing manuals and guidelines for mainstreaming social accountability in health care service delivery systems. As the first head of Kenya's Health Sector Services Fund, through which the country's government and development partners pool funds, he was responsible for capacity building to allow facilities to receive direct funding for improvement of services, while maintaining strong accountability mechanisms through engagement with citizens.

Eva Ombaka, senior lecturer at St. John's University of Tanzania, trained as a pharmacist in England and received both her Ph.D. and master's degree in public health from institutions in the UK. She has worked in hospital practice, academia, and manufacturing. For half of her 37-year career, she was involved in policy development and capacity building for better pharmaceutical practice. Her main areas of interest are access to medicines and the promotion of their rational use. She has participated in courses and committees addressing different aspects of access to and use of medicines in organizations such as the World Health Organization and Health Action International, and is an active member of MSG-Pharma, the multistakeholder coalition in Tanzania. In her former capacity as coordinator of the Ecumenical Pharmaceutical Network, and as founder and board member of the Sustainable Health Care Foundation, Ombaka actively supported participative research and networking as effective ways of learning and sharing best practices.

Teresa Omondi is currently the deputy executive director of the Federation of Women Lawyers (FIDA) Kenya, which advocates—among other things—reproductive health rights for women. A lawyer with over 10 years' experience in governance and human rights, she is a founding member of FoTAPP. Prior to joining FIDA, she was deputy executive director of Transparency International's Kenya chapter. Before that she served as executive director of the Gender Violence Recovery Centre at Nairobi Women's Hospital.

Abbreviations

AFIC	Africa Freedom of Information Center
AIDS	acquired immune deficiency syndrome
COMESA	Common Market for Eastern and Southern Africa
CoST	Construction Sector Transparency Initiative
CSO	Civil Society Organization
DANIDA	Danish International Development Agency
DFID	Department for International Development (UK)
EITI	Extractive Industries Transparency Initiative
ERP	Enterprise Resource Program
FBOs	faith-based organizations
FKPM	Federation of Kenya Pharmaceutical Manufacturers
FoTAPP	Forum for Transparency and Accountability in Pharmaceutical Procurement
GDP	gross domestic product
GOe	Global Observatory for eHealth
HAI	Health Action International
HAI-Africa	Health Action International-Africa
HEPS	Coalition for Health Promotion and Social Development
HIV	human immunodeficiency virus
HSSIP	Health Sector Strategic Investment Plan
HSSP	Health Sector Strategic Plan
HUMC	Health Unit Management Committee
ICT	Information and Communications Technology
JMS	Joint Medical Store
KAM	Kenya Association of Manufacturers
KAPI	Kenya Association of Pharmaceutical Industry
KEML	Kenya Essential Medicines List
KEMSA	Kenya Medical Supplies Agency

KEPSA	Kenya Private Sector Alliance
KHF	Kenya Health Federation
LGA	Local Government Authority
LMIS	Logistics Management Information System
MDG	Millennium Development Goal
MDTS	Mobile-Phone Drug Tracking System
M&E	monitoring and evaluation
MEDS	Mission for Essential Drugs and Supplies
MeTA	Medicines Transparency Alliance
MHSW	Ministry of Health and Social Welfare, Tanzania
MoH	Ministry of Health
MoU	Memorandum of Understanding
MSD	Medical Stores Department
MSG	Multistakeholder Group
MSG-Pharma	Multistakeholder Group on Pharmaceutical Procurement
MSH	Management Sciences for Health
NDA	National Drug Authority
NGO	nongovernmental organization
NMS	National Medical Store
NPSSP	National Pharmaceutical Sector Strategic Plan
NTA	National Taxpayers Association
PDA	personal digital assistants
PMU	Procurement Management Unit
PPB	Pharmacy and Poisons Board
PPDA	Public Procurement and Disposal of Assets Authority
PPDPA	Public Procurement Disposal of Public Assets Authority
PPOA	Public Procurement Oversight Authority, Kenya
PPPH	Public Private Partnership for Health
PPRA	Public Procurement Regulatory Authority, Tanzania
PSK	Pharmaceutical Society of Kenya
PSM	pharmaceutical procurement and supply chain management
PWG	Pharmaceutical Working Group
STG	Standard Treatment Guidelines
SWAP	sector-wide approach
TEITI	Tanzania Extractive Industries Transparency Initiative
TFDA	Tanzania Food and Drugs Authority
TI Kenya	Transparency International, Kenya Chapter
ToT	training of trainers

TRIPS	Trade-Related Intellectual Property Services
UHC	universal health coverage
UNHCO	Uganda National Health Consumers' Organization
UNICEF	United Nations Children's Fund
USAID	United States Agency for International Development
WBI	World Bank Institute
WHO	World Health Organization
YLL	years of life lost

CHAPTER 1

Background

Yvonne Nkrumah and Julia Mensah

Introduction

Today more than ever, most countries are reforming their health systems in an effort to provide health care that is equitable, affordable, and of good quality. This quest for universal health coverage (UHC) is expected to dominate the post-Millennium Development Goal (MDG) agenda and is also viewed as being central to the attainment of the "right to health",[1] the elimination of extreme poverty, and the boosting of shared prosperity. These are collectively necessary to promote social inclusion, accelerate socioeconomic development, and enhance quality of life, especially for the poor.

UHC aims to guarantee access to health care services without placing an extreme financial burden on patients, particularly vulnerable groups. In this sense, it protects users from financial ruin or impoverishment. Though noble in concept, UHC presents several challenges, including how to broaden access to services and health commodities, notably essential medicines.

Without improved access to medicines, UHC will make very limited advancements. This is because medicines—when needed—constitute a large proportion of household expenditures. In developing economies, 50 percent of health care costs are financed through out-of-pocket expenses. An estimated 68 percent of these out-of-pocket health costs are for medicines (Management Sciences for Health 2012). Expenditure on medicines therefore has the potential to drive households into financial ruin and impoverishment. Yet the World Health Organization (WHO) estimates that about 30 percent of the world's population—approximately 2 billion people—still lacks regular access to essential medicines. In the poorest parts of Africa and Asia, this figure rises to over 50 percent.

Countries are implementing several types of reform and initiative aimed at making life-saving medicines readily available and affordable to the poor. One

The authors wish to acknowledge Richard Crabbe for the extensive research and background information that helped shape the initial draft.

area of increased focus is strengthening the governance—transparency and accountability—of pharmaceutical procurement and supply chain management (PSM). This is because PSM entails complex processes, is multifaceted, and involves many stakeholders, including government agencies, procurement agencies, manufacturers, distributors, health facilities, and citizens. As a result of this complexity, it tends to be especially prone to inefficiency and corruption. Poor governance in PSM contributes to overpriced products, leakages, stock-outs, and oversupply or waste.

Management Sciences for Health[2] notes that five of the 10 leading causes of waste in health systems relate directly to pharmaceuticals. WHO also estimates that, on average, African governments pay 34–44 percent more for medicines than necessary. So, how do countries do more and better with limited resources? Could greater transparency and accountability in PSM help reduce waste and enhance access to medicines? What is the potential for collaborative action in effectively addressing these challenges?

Governance in PSM: A Crucial Role

Governance has been identified as being crucial for universal access to health care and for health sector performance. It was defined as a priority area of work in the WHO Medicines Strategy 2008–13.[3] WHO defines good governance in pharmaceuticals as "the formulation and implementation of appropriate policies and procedures that ensure the effective, efficient, and ethical management of pharmaceutical systems, in particular medicine regulatory systems and medicine supply systems, in a manner that is transparent, accountable, follows the rule of law and minimizes corruption" (Aniello 2008).

Transparency and accountability are key cornerstones of good governance. Lack of transparency and accountability not only results in corruption and the waste of scarce development resources, but also severely compromises the quality and effectiveness of public policy making, planning, and the provision of services to meet basic needs. It denies citizens their inherent right to influence decisions that directly affect their lives and to hold governments accountable for the public resources with which they are entrusted.

Well-performing pharmaceutical procurement systems and supply chains are fundamental to ensuring good quality medicines are available, affordable, and accessible to patients. To improve lives on a large scale, it is especially important that limited resources are fully utilized in order to ensure value for money, and to improve access to medicines. Reducing unnecessary expenditure on medicines, using them more appropriately and improving quality control could save countries up to 5 percent of their health expenditure (World Health Organization 2011).

Common governance weaknesses in procurement include a lack of access to information, poor enforcement and implementation of policies and regulations, a lack of capacity to formulate reliable estimates, and an inability to ensure that proper incentives are in place to lessen the likelihood of corruption at both individual and institutional levels (World Health Organization 2011). Procedural weaknesses lengthen procurement lead time and delivery delays. Diversion, leakages, and wasteful mismanagement are also observed in public sector medicine supply chains. Despite considerable efforts to identify and remedy poor governance at national level, countries continue to face major challenges in the reform process.

The Case for Collective Action

While government, private sector, and civil society actors acknowledge the challenges in PSM, each group has tended to address these problems on its own, with minimal engagement between them. The direct result of this approach has been poorly coordinated efforts leading to unsustainable reforms and the perpetuation of poor outcomes in health service delivery—particularly around access to essential medicines.

Collective action refers to the process through which individuals and groups work together toward a shared vision and attaining a common goal (Cabañero-Verzosa and Garcia 2011). Multistakeholder processes are essential because they bring together different actors who have a shared interest in a problem, and engage them in dialogue and collective learning that can improve innovation, decision making, and action. These processes promote better participatory decision making by ensuring that the views of key actors—from government, the private sector, civil society, and the media—are heard and integrated at all stages, through dialogue and consensus building.

Global experience demonstrates that among the available options for collective action and collaborative engagement, building coalitions is one of the most effective for achieving common objectives (Cabañero-Verzosa and Garcia 2011). Cabañero-Verzosa and Garcia define coalitions as "structures of formal collaboration undergirded by a common vision, and facilitate shared decision-making, material resources among individuals, groups, and organizations. They are formed to carry out joint or coordinated activities and can be either a time-bound or open-ended partnership to achieve a common purpose" (p. 280).

Cohen, Baer, and Satterwhite (2002) point out that coalitions offer numerous potential advantages over working independently. The broader purpose and breadth of coalitions make them more powerful than individual organizations. They build trust and consensus between people and organizations that have a shared vision and common goal. In addition, they reduce suspicion of self-interest; accomplish objectives beyond the scope of any single organization; achieve more widespread reach within a community than any single organization could attain, and can foster cooperation between grassroots organizations, community members, and diverse sectors of a large organization.

When a change process is needed to address a complex problem, it is necessary to assess what type of multistakeholder coalition-building approach would be most appropriate to solve the problem. This calls for identifying the right range of processes, mobilizing the various constituents, and supporting them through capacity development that would help them achieve their objective.

Improving PSM Governance: The Initiative

As part of the drive to increase efficiency in the use of resources and improve health outcomes through better governance in PSM, the World Bank Institute (WBI) has launched a multiyear capacity-building initiative: Improving Governance in Pharmaceutical Procurement and Supply Chain Management. This brings together multiple stakeholders involved in PSM to forge consensus on governance challenges, identify areas for action and improvement, initiate peer-to-peer learning, and facilitate the implementation of measures to improve transparency and accountability in pharmaceutical PSM. It approaches governance from both the demand and supply sides by focusing on multistakeholder dialogue as a key component of its strategy. Unique to this approach is the inclusion and participation of a wide range of stakeholders, with a view to developing country level multistakeholder groups (MSGs) that can drive change.

The initiative was developed through extensive consultation with clients, practitioners, Bank Task Team Leaders, and key development partners to ensure synergy with broader efforts to strengthen health systems. It recognizes that improving transparency and accountability in PSM is a continuous, long-term process requiring technical expertise, leadership skills, and transformative coalition and capacity building. In 2010, WBI launched the initiative in Kenya, Tanzania, and Uganda. These countries make excellent candidates for the program, as they have been pioneers in reforming PSM processes and have the capacity to build on these reforms through collaborative multistakeholder engagement to influence policy action.

The initiative provides an innovative solution by bringing stakeholders together to prioritize collectively key areas where critical action is required but lacking, and supporting them to develop action plans for joint implementation. Working through a national convener, coalitions implement a set of activities linked to their strategic objectives and defined in their action plans, thereby ensuring incremental progress toward the attainment of their common goals.

The initiative aims to contribute to improving access to essential medicines in the three countries by strengthening the capacity of multistakeholder coalitions comprising public and private sector actors involved in PSM, and civil society organizations (CSOs)—including academia, the media, and faith-based organizations—to work collectively in improving transparency, accountability, and efficiency in PSM. The goal is to leverage the strengths of different stakeholders by enabling the creation of comprehensive and unified strategies, facilitating information sharing across interest groups, improving data collection and reporting, monitoring public procurement and supply chain systems, and establishing mutual accountability for results. The initiative does not intend to replicate efforts by other partners focused on enhancing the technical or institutional capacity of medicine procurement agencies. Rather, it seeks to complement these efforts by fostering better collaboration between policy makers, service providers, and demand-side actors to promote transparency, accountability, and efficiency in PSM.

The consultative approach provided through multistakeholder coalitions helps ensure broader dialogue on reform priorities, forges consensus around strategic measures, leverages strengths and expertise (as well as intellectual and social capital in the attainment of desired outcomes), and generates greater buy-in and ownership of change processes at the country level. This helps ensure greater sustainability and the potential for transformative impact.

Through capacity development, WBI has provided the coalitions with cutting-edge tools to build strong relationships across stakeholder groups, understand and manage the political economy of reforms, enhance technical understanding of PSM issues, and engage demand-side actors in generating evidence-based data to inform policy making. These capacity development components are intended to strengthen collaborative action toward reforms and are, in turn, expected to accelerate PSM change processes and ultimately improve access to medicines. Tanzania, Kenya, and Uganda have initiated country-level processes that have the potential to enhance governance in pharmaceutical procurement and supply chain management. Through an online community of practice, http://www.enepp.net, the coalitions share experiences, cross-pollinate ideas, and engage in peer-to-peer learning.

Why This Book?

Drawing on these experiences, this book is written primarily by and for practitioners interested in building coalitions for collective action. Chapters 2, 3, and 4 are authored by representatives of multistakeholder coalitions in Tanzania, Kenya, and Uganda, respectively. These chapters provide an insider perspective on the processes of developing and sustaining a coalition, as well as leveraging resources (human and financial) and galvanizing buy-in to implement collective, results-oriented interventions aimed at achieving coalition members' shared vision. The authors provide real and practical examples of opportunities and challenges, as well as insightful lessons learned from the process in each country. These practical experiences demonstrate that multistakeholder approaches require a demanding mix of technical expertise, funding, outreach, and sustained commitment to overcome challenges—but they also show that coalitions have powerful potential to bring important health system benefits to governments and the citizens they serve.

Outline of the Book

After this introductory chapter, subsequent chapters are set out to present coalition building in the form of a tree—roots, trunk, and branches. The roots signify the origins and initial steps taken to build a coalition and the associated teething problems; the trunk represents efforts toward sustaining the organization's existence and growth; and the branches highlight the collective actions undertaken by the coalition in fulfillment of its aims and objectives. In preparing this book, and based on their unique experiences, Tanzania, Kenya, and Uganda respectively focus their chapters on the roots, trunk, and branches. To further the tree analogy, each country's chapter draws parallels or makes comparisons with what pertains in the other two countries, to show how they benefit from each other in an ongoing knowledge exchange.

Chapter 2 (Putting Down Roots, Tanzania) has three main sections: an overview of the country context and health reform agenda; a discussion of the experiences of MSG-Pharma, Tanzania's multistakeholder body, in setting up a coalition, and lessons learned. These outline the reasons leading to the establishment of the multistakeholder group and describe how challenges met during its formation stages were overcome.

Chapter 3 (Growing a Strong Trunk, Kenya) provides insights into the approaches employed by Kenya's multistakeholder coalition, the Forum for Transparency and Accountability in Pharmaceutical Procurement (FoTAPP), in order to sustain the interest and commitment of key stakeholders. It presents a brief description of the Kenyan context in relation to the pharmaceutical sector, highlighting challenges in the sector, and the importance of a multistakeholder coalition amid other reform platforms.

Chapter 4 (Branching Out and Bearing Fruits, Uganda) describes the opportunities, challenges, and rewards associated with designing and implementing a joint intervention in furtherance of the goals of the Medicines Transparency Alliance (MeTA), the coalition in Uganda. It also illustrates how the coalition has been able to inform policy dialogue and reform efforts in the health sector.

Notes

1. The Universal Declaration of Human Rights encapsulates the most widely accepted normative standard for the "right to health". It declares that each person has the right to a standard of living adequate for the health and well-being of themselves and of their family. This includes the rights to food, clothing, housing, medical care, and necessary social services, as well as the right to the highest attainable standard of physical and mental health.

2. Management Sciences for Health (http://www.msh.org) works with health leaders throughout the world on global health's biggest challenges, with a focus on human immunodeficiency virus (HIV) and acquired immune deficiency syndrome (AIDS), tuberculosis (TB), malaria, chronic diseases, family planning, and maternal and child health.

3. The need for good governance in the pharmaceutical sector: http://www.who.int/ medicines/areas/governance/en/ (accessed April 14, 2014).

CHAPTER 2

Putting Down Roots
Establishing a Multistakeholder Group and Building Consensus: Lessons from Tanzania

Jacqueline Idusso, Joseph Mhando, and Eva Ombaka

Introduction

The creation of a multistakeholder group involves several intricate processes that have to be managed carefully to ensure broad-based support, as well as long-term sustainability. This chapter, based primarily on the experiences of the Tanzania Multistakeholder Group on Pharmaceutical Procurement ("MSG-Pharma"), discusses the approach used to develop a local coalition and shares some of the key lessons learned from the process. It also draws on the rich experiences of the multistakeholder groups in Kenya and Uganda.

This chapter has three main sections:

- An overview of the country context and health reform agenda
- A discussion of MSG-Pharma's own experiences in setting up a coalition
- Lessons learned.

These outline the reasons leading to the establishment of the multistakeholder group and describe how challenges met during its formation stages were overcome—a process which yielded several key lessons, as indicated in box 2.1 below:

Box 2.1 Key Lessons in the Establishment of a Multistakeholder Group: Tanzania

1. Setting up a coalition requires the mobilization of stakeholders with a common understanding of the reform agenda and a shared vision for achieving results. Such unified vision establishes an important basis around which different actors—despite their varying interests—can rally.

---

box continues next page

Box 2.1   Key Lessons in the Establishment of a Multistakeholder Group: Tanzania *(continued)*

2. A thorough stakeholder mapping is always necessary at the formation stage of a coalition in order to ensure that the appropriate players—who are credible, legitimate, and influential—are involved and can bring their individual strengths to bear.

3. In voluntary groups, such as the multistakeholder coalitions in Tanzania, Kenya, and Uganda, it can be difficult to sustain membership interest and commitment. Members tend to be active around issues directly relevant to their own strategic interests. Coalitions therefore need to be flexible and understand the inherently dynamic nature of such a group. They should make appropriate provision to evolve their activities and priorities based on inevitable changes in membership interests and levels of commitment.

4. Stakeholders must recognize that there is no "one-size-fits-all" coalition. In some contexts "networks" may be more appropriate, while in others a more structured process or entity is required.

5. It is important to codify the rules of engagement in the coalition so that all members understand clearly what is required of them.

This chapter also discusses challenges related to governance issues in procurement and supply chain management in the pharmaceutical sector.

Tanzania Country Context

Tanzania's population is predominantly young and rural, and is growing fast. In 2012, it was estimated at 47.7 million people, with 45 percent aged 0–14 (Tanzania Demographics Profile 2013). Only 27 percent of Tanzanians live in urban areas (UNICEF 2012). The country's disease burden consists largely of communicable diseases, which comprised 78 percent of years of life lost (YLL) in 2008. Non-communicable diseases comprised 13 percent of YLL and injuries contributed to 8 percent (World Health Organization [WHO] 2014). Malaria and human immunodeficiency virus (HIV) and acquired immune deficiency syndrome (AIDS) are key contributors to Tanzania's communicable disease burden. Other such diseases include tuberculosis and neglected tropical diseases such as schistosomiasis, soil-transmitted helminthes, lymphatic filariasis, onchocerciasis, and trachoma (WHO Regional Office for Africa 2009).

Mainland Tanzania has 25 regions and 133 local authorities, with health services reflecting these administrative divisions. Since the early 2000s, the Ministry of Health and Social Welfare (MHSW) has been implementing health system reform programs. These have historically focused on decentralization, financial reforms, public-private partnerships, and the integration of vertical health programs into general health services. The most critical health system challenges currently facing the country include weak pharmaceutical procurement and supply chain management, resulting in high levels of stock-outs; a human resources crisis comprising a shortage of staff and a lack of skills; a fragmented health information system, and underfunding and poor resource allocation in health care financing.

Key Health Issues and the Reform Agenda

The Health Sector Strategic Plan III[1]

In 2010, the third phase of the government's umbrella Health Sector Strategic Plan (HSSP III) was implemented. Within this were two major programs: the Primary Health Services Development Program and the Human Resources for Health Strategic Plan. These programs were aimed at improving access to and the quality of health services, in order to help Tanzania meet the Millennium Development Goals (MDGs). The programs were regarded as key in improving the health of the population. In order to support them, the focus of the HSSP III was on partnership.

For example, under the government's Decentralization by Devolution policy, Local Government Authorities (LGAs) were in charge of delivering social services. The Regional Administration and Local Government department of the prime minister's office was tasked with monitoring and coordinating the LGAs' activities, in line with sectoral ministries' policies and guidelines. Other ministries, departments, and agencies were also required to support the MHSW in improving the population's health, through education, agriculture, or water supply, for example. This sector-wide approach (SWAP)[2] required the health sector to work in partnership with all government institutions responsible for services that impact on health.

Partnership with the private sector was also considered necessary to increase access to and the quality of health services. In this context, the private sector consists of all nonstate actors, including nongovernmental organizations (NGOs), faith-based organizations, community-based organizations, and other private health providers. The service agreements between the government and private service providers offer opportunities for regulated collaboration, while development partners provide the health sector with the needed financial and technical support. In 2008, a new Memorandum of Understanding (MoU) was signed for the Health Basket Fund—a donor-based funding mechanism initiated in 1999 as part of the Tanzanian Government's decision to pursue SWAP in the health sector. SWAP is well-established in Tanzania and offers all partners an opportunity to contribute to better health nationwide. The HSSP III has 11 specific objectives. These mainly target improvements in access to health services, better use of resources, and encouragement of public-private partnerships.

Key Challenges in the Pharmaceutical Sector

Access to essential medicines is usually regarded as a key indicator of success in health care systems. In Tanzania, as in other parts of the world, medicines have variable and often high prices, and are unaffordable for large sections of the population. The high burden of paying for essential medicines falls disproportionately on poor households, resulting in preventable morbidity and mortality. However, the issue of improving access to medicines is complex and extends far beyond their availability, and even beyond the health care system. Many different factors and causes must be taken into account and targeted.

The HSSP III recognizes that the disbursement of funds for medicines and supplies has been irregular and less than pledged in budget allocation. Capacity to forecast and quantify needs in public health facilities at all levels is low. In some facilities, storage conditions for medicines are poor. The shortage of qualified pharmaceutical staff is critical in both public and private sectors, and irrational use of pharmaceuticals and medical supplies remains a challenge. An inadequate transport system at district level affects peripheral distribution of pharmaceuticals and medicine supplies, as well as management supervision (Tanzania Health Sector Strategic Plan III).

Organization of Pharmaceutical Functions

In Tanzania, several agencies have a role in the procurement and supply chain management of medicines. The Ministry of Health and Social Welfare (MHSW) supervises procurement through its Pharmaceutical Services Unit. The Medical Stores Department (MSD) is an autonomous department of the MHSW responsible for the procurement, storage, and distribution of medicines. Regulation to ensure the quality and efficacy of medicines is the primary responsibility of the Tanzania Food and Drugs Authority (TFDA). The Public Procurement Regulatory Authority (PPRA) is an agency vested with oversight of all public procurements, including medicines.

The National Essential Medicines List of Tanzania and Standard Treatment Guidelines, last published in 1997, were both updated in 2006 and 2013 in order to reflect changes in current medical knowledge and practice. They aim to enable both MSD and health workers to know what treatments are recommended, at which level, and which medicines are considered essential and must therefore be procured. MSD is the main supplier of pharmaceuticals to the public sector, and the primary supplier to faith-based and other nongovernment, noncommercial groups providing health services in Tanzania.

The Role of Local Government Authorities and the Medicine Supply System

In the context of the national health system, Tanzania's administrative districts have been identified as the focal point for ongoing health sector reforms. Since 2003, the country's five-year Health Sector Strategic Plans have emphasized the district health component as being the level closest to communities and at which most essential health services are provided.

The central government allocates operational funds for district-level health services based on the number and level of health facilities in each local authority. Government funds for the supply of medicines are deposited at MSD, from which health facilities procure medicines by requisition. Complementary funds for procuring medicines can be made available from a district's own funds, insurance schemes, patient contribution schemes, and multilateral sources (so-called "basket funds"). According to the Health Sector Public Expenditure Review for 2011, complementary health financing continues to grow, and the main challenge facing health service funds is to use accumulated monies to improve health services, instead of holding large reserves (Pharmaceutical Services Unit 2012). Figure 2.1 below illustrates the system.

Challenges in the Procurement of Medicines

Public procurement in Tanzania is currently governed by the Public Procurement Act 2004 (revised 2011). This requires the establishment of a procurement unit and a tender committee in each procurement entity, such as a local council. To enhance transparency in the purchasing process, procurement entities are required to publish annual procurement plans at the beginning of each fiscal year. Each district has been provided with procurement, stores, and pharmaceutical staff deemed sufficient to discharge the relevant procurement functions.

In spite of these arrangements, several challenges affect medicine procurement and supply chain management in Tanzania. At the national level, these include weak quantification and procurement planning; poor human resource development, and deployment; inadequate disclosure of information; weak coordination among agencies involved in the procurement process, and weak accountability systems. Medicine procurement at district level was in the past restricted to items provided by the MSD. However, non-MSD procurement of medical supplies has recently become significant due to increased funds being generated through health financing schemes: community health funds, national health insurance funds, and patient contribution schemes. Unfortunately, at district level, non-MSD procurement is prone to exploitation, due to inadequate controls and weak procedures. Although the Public Procurement Act introduced extensive processes aimed at streamlining and directing procurement procedures in all public

Figure 2.1 The Medicines Supply System in Tanzania

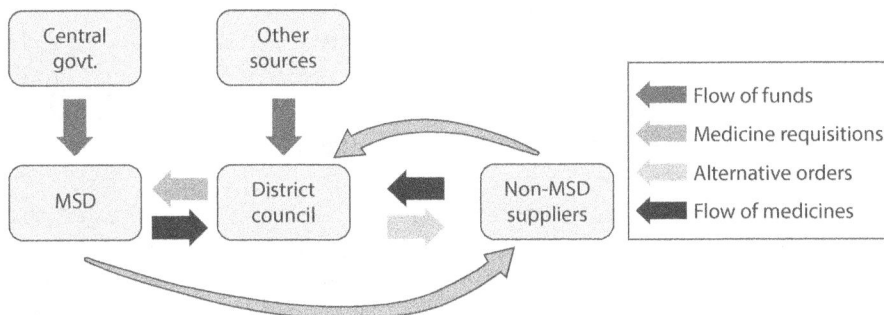

Source: World Bank.
Note: Arrows indicate the alternative supply route that should be ideally used when stocks are not available at MSD.
MSD = Medical Stores Department.

institutions, compliance at district level is still very poor. Key reasons (World Bank Institute 2013) include the following:

- Inadequate human resource capacity for procurement units in some districts
- Nonadherence to procurement laws and regulations
- Poor quantification at district level
- Inadequate planning capacity.

The procurement of medicines could benefit from improvements in various areas relating to policy and regulatory framework, quantification, procurement processes, institutional arrangements, and disclosure of information. Although the majority of these areas are being addressed through institutional strengthening and technical capacity development, third-party monitoring could also play a crucial role in ensuring that the procurement of medicines is conducted in an efficient and transparent manner, delivering the best value for money and improving performance.

Rationale for Setting up a Multistakeholder Coalition

An initial rapid country assessment[3] to understand strengths and weaknesses in Tanzania's medicine procurement system validated most of the challenges outlined above. The assessment provided a clear picture of the procurement system, as well as the mechanisms in place to ensure transparency and accountability, the extent to which these mechanisms are used, and their levels of effectiveness. It confirmed that problems in pharmaceutical procurement are widespread and well recognized, but have proved resistant to piecemeal efforts at improvement. At a validation meeting to discuss the findings of the country assessment (attended by nearly 20 participants from government agencies, academia, the donor community, and other stakeholder groups), it became evident that collaborative action was necessary in order to solve these complex challenges.

Multistakeholder coalitions are largely recognized for their ability to solve complex problems by interactive learning processes. To start the process and spur stakeholders into action, participants at the validation workshop committed to establishing a multistakeholder group (MSG-Pharma). Several key reasons were behind the decision. The magnitude of the problems meant that no single group could address them alone, while levels of linkage and possible conflict between different players had the potential to derail any attempts to do so. These needed to be taken into account through group action.

Working in coalition is also synergistic, drawing on players' different strengths. For example, civil society organizations (CSOs) often know the community well and can interact with lay people, while health care providers can interact at institutional level. The multistakeholder process is also empowering, providing the whole group with greater influence, resources, and knowledge based on individual members' different strengths. Members are more likely to be heard, as different audiences can identify with different group members and a multistakeholder group does not appear as a sector interest group. It also helps members to hold one another accountable, in that actions agreed together are more likely to be carried out.

The overall objective of MSG-Pharma is to strengthen transparency and accountability in pharmaceutical procurement, in order to increase efficiency in the use of resources and help improve access to medicines. Given the country assessment findings, the group's initial focus was on central procurement at MSD, but it later opted to concentrate on strengthening the role of CSOs in the inter-action between service providers and end-users. This implied a shift of attention from central to district-level procurement. The choice was prompted by the realization that resources for procurement of medicines outside MSD had increased significantly at the district level. Monitoring and strengthening district-level procurement processes would therefore generate more value, more quickly, contributing significantly toward increasing access to essential medicines in the short term. This shift of attention from central to district-level procurement was also more aligned to HSSP III and the priorities of the Public Procurement Regulatory Authority (PPRA), which at the time was keen to collaborate with CSOs and other stakeholders to monitor adherence to procurement policies and procedures at the district level.

MSG-Pharma consequently prioritized district-level procurement of medi-cines through monitoring procurement inputs (planning), the procurement process (contract award and implementation), outputs (price and stock), and service delivery (through citizen monitoring). An important component of this would be the use of collected information to design interventions to improve service delivery.

Multistakeholder Groups and Other Forms of Collaboration in Tanzania before 2010

Tanzania emerged from one-party rule in 1995, under which access to informa-tion and freedom of speech were greatly curtailed. As a result, when the multi-stakeholder approach to enhancing governance made its debut in the country, civil society activity was still nascent. Collaboration between civil society and other sectors often involved state sponsorship, political activism, and international patronage. For example, the Tanzania Extractive Industries Transparency Initiative (TEITI) was modelled on the principles of the Extractive Industries Transparency Initiative (EITI), a global coalition of governments, companies, and civil society working together to improve open and accountable management of revenues from natural resources. TEITI has an equal balance of participants from govern-ment, the private sector, and civil society, and was established in February 2009 by the government, as required by EITI.

Another coalition, the Construction Sector Transparency Initiative (CoST), was formed in 2008 to provide for the disclosure of construction project information. The initiative aims to ensure that sufficient information is provided for stakeholders to make informed judgments about the cost and quality of construction projects. Disclosures include a description of the project, its purpose and location, and summary details of the original and final project specifications, cost, contractors, and completion dates. The disclosures also include justification for any significant differences between the original and final information, as well as project evaluation and completion reports. According to the coalition's website, the champion of CoST is the minister responsible for good governance, who is expected "to use her or his strategic position to help overcome challenges facing the project". The CoST multistakeholder group is made up of two members from civil society, four from the private sector, and six from the public sector.

These two multistakeholder groups established before 2010 exhibited strong elements of state patronage and had calculated civil society engagement. However, according to a report published by NGOs in 2011, Tanzania has a sizeable civil society made up of cooperatives, faith-based organizations, community-based organizations, informal grassroots organizations, the independent media, and issue-based groups (for example, gender, age-based, or representing people with disabilities). There were also groups active on key social issues including poverty, HIV and AIDS, education, and health (Civil Society Profile: Tanzania). The most common forms of collaboration among civil society groups at that time were associations and networks that fostered cooperation for building capacity and enhancing legitimacy. According to the report, there were at least 228 networks, 59 percent of which were defined by specific themes, the rest more general. At least 170 networks were district specific, while 25 were subnational and 33 national. At that time, civil society was perceived as having successfully influenced gender rights and human rights, with less influence on transparency, one of Tanzania's major challenges. The global anticorruption NGO Transparency International does not have a chapter in Tanzania (Transparency International 2014).

Collaborations in the Health and Pharmaceutical Sectors

In addition to civil society associations active in the health sector, development partners also played an important role in supporting and monitoring government activities while demanding accountability through the Health Basket Fund. The basket is funded by a number of development agencies which pool unrestricted resources to support the implementation of HSSP III. By 2010 there were seven development partners contributing to the Health Basket Fund: Canada, Denmark, Ireland, Switzerland, the United Nations (UN) Population Fund, United Nations Children's Fund (UNICEF), and the World Bank (Development Partners Group Tanzania).

Channeling resources through such a mechanism confirms a commitment toward a more effective and efficient use of aid, in line with both the Paris

Declaration and the aspirations of the Tanzanian government, as elaborated in the Joint Assistance Strategy. The Health SWAP Committee provides a forum for consultations and the exchange of ideas and experiences between the different health sector stakeholders. The committee has several working groups, including the Pharmaceutical Working Group (PWG), which was added in acknowledgment of the problems facing the pharmaceutical sector in the country. The working group supports government efforts to achieve the objectives of the National Medicine Policy, which aims at "making available to all Tanzanians at all times the essential pharmaceutical products which are of quality, proven effectiveness, and acceptable safety, at a price that the individual and the community can afford, when they are needed to prevent, cure, or reduce illness and suffering" (Pharmaceutical Working Group). The working group provides sound advice and technical support for sustainable improvement of the pharmaceutical sector. Membership is based on institutional representation, with a designated focal person expected to participate in group activities.

Learning from Other Countries

Experience in neighboring countries offered the Multistakeholder Group (MSG) useful lessons. In Uganda, a precedent was set by the successful collaboration between the World Health Organization (WHO), Health Action International-Africa (HAI-Africa), and the Ministry of Health to monitor the price and availability of medicines. The Medicines Transparency Alliance (MeTA) is a coalition comprising stakeholders from the government (National Medical Stores, the National Drug Authority and the Ministry of Health), professional associations such as the Pharmaceutical Society of Uganda, the private sector (such as Medical Access Uganda Limited, Surgipharm, and Kampala Pharmaceutical Industries), and CSOs. The Ministry of Health chose the multistakeholder approach as a means of effectively countering the mutual suspicion that existed among stakeholders in the pharmaceutical sector, arising from their different interests and leading to a blame game. The government was blamed for not doing enough, CSOs were considered to be "making noise for no reason", while private sector players suspected they were not being sufficiently involved and that information was not being disclosed to them, to their detriment. This necessitated the establishment of a "safe space" to foster a meeting of minds in an unambiguous manner, given that the different stakeholders had different perspectives on access to medicines and could bring their respective competencies to enhance policy dialogue at the Ministry of Health.

MeTA Uganda was established with funding from the United Kingdom's Department for International Development (DFID). A mapping study was conducted by the International MeTA Secretariat to identify stakeholders from the private sector—pharmaceutical manufacturers, associations, importers, and distributors. Once the right people were brought together around the table, administrative structures were formed. These included the MeTA Council—a wide representation of stakeholder voices in the pharmaceutical sector led by three co-chairs drawn from different stakeholder groups on a rotating basis. A secretariat was also established, consisting of representatives from the government, the private sector, and civil society, led by a coordinator.

The benefits of this approach are many. The coalition has provided an umbrella organization for CSOs and a platform for gaining audience with other stakeholders and for continuous dialogue. This in itself helps build capacity. The CSOs are now better organized and coordinated and their capacity has been developed to enable them present their issues in a more professional and businesslike manner. The private sector also receives regular communications about issues and developments in the sector.

The Need for a Different Multistakeholder Approach in Tanzania

After a review of the situation in Tanzania in 2010 and the learning from MeTA's experience, it became clear that the Tanzanian context was unique, owing to several key characteristics:

- Lack of health activism, despite widespread citizen dissatisfaction with health service delivery
- Lack of CSO engagement in procurement monitoring
- The existence of state-sponsored collaborations in politically sensitive operations, for example, mining and construction
- The presence of a development partners' forum that sought to monitor government activity and control its expenditure pattern by diplomatic means
- Civil society associations that focused on capacity building and legitimacy
- Weak anticorruption activity.

The situation demanded intervention in the form of civil society monitoring of health commodity procurement, with relevance and value for money as central themes. Such intervention would augment efforts by development partners and others to monitor government activity through budget controls. As such an approach was pioneering in nature, multistakeholder collaboration was necessary to bring together primary stakeholders for dialogue, decision making, and implementation of solutions to common problems and goals. Monitoring of pharmaceutical procurement using simple indicators was considered easy to implement and capable of producing quick results that could later be extended to other health and nonhealth areas.

Lacking previous experience in the multistakeholder approach, participants anticipated challenges such as the following:

- Low appreciation of the benefits of working in a multistakeholder group
- A perceived challenge to existing modes of collaboration
- Lack of internal champions
- Lack of funds.

Based on the Ugandan experience, it was obvious that many challenges would arise when the coalition began to operate, but that these would be far outweighed by the benefits. Specific safeguards against these challenges would be necessary in deciding the administrative structure and during the implementation of the initiative.

With this in mind, Tanzania chose a different administrative approach from MeTA, establishing a loose coalition, MSG-Pharma, which offers its members more freedom to participate depending on current activities. Instead of establishing a permanent formal secretariat, Tanzania chose to work under steering committees and secretariats hosted by a member organization. This arrangement provided the fluidity necessary for a coalition of the willing. It was also a less costly administrative structure than a permanent secretariat (Tanzania lacked the financial support from DFID and technical expertise from MeTA International which Uganda enjoyed).

In Kenya, as in Uganda and Tanzania, several international and national organizations previously working separately in health care came together to form the Forum for Transparency and Accountability in Pharmaceutical Procurement (FoTAPP).

From Dispersed Groups to Coalition

The stakeholders knew the issues to be addressed, knew what was needed, and knew something of the process. The question remained: how best to start a coalition from scratch?

Mapping the Stakeholders

Once it was clear that a multistakeholder group was a viable option for addressing pharmaceutical procurement issues, it became necessary to identify and bring together potential members. Unlike Uganda, where MeTA existed, or neighboring Kenya, where the convener (Transparency International) used its own database to invite potential members to the coalition's founding meeting, the process in Tanzania started with a desk review and interviews of key players. This helped to identify which groups and individuals were working on issues directly or indirectly linked to pharmaceutical procurement and gave in-depth understanding of the country situation.

The process provided a draft list of stakeholders, which contained diverse groups. The first included members with significant political power, including government ministries, agencies, or departments such as the Tanzania Food and Drugs Authority (TFDA), MSD, and the MHSW procurement unit, as well as representatives of the donor community. Although the procurement of medicine falls under their mandates, their involvement in the coalition can be limited by political changes and the availability of time. For example, during the coalition-building exercise, the Minister of Health and other key leaders in MHSW were replaced. Consequently, the coordinator paid a courtesy call on the new appointees as soon as they assumed office and informed them about MSG-Pharma. The temporary nature of political appointments would necessitate frequent reestablishment of relationships with policy makers and key decision makers.

A second group was the business community, including suppliers, manufacturers, importers, retailers, and their associations. This group has financial power and an interest in maximizing profits legally. The third group comprised professional bodies, such as doctors' and pharmacists' associations, academic institutions, and not-for-profit service providers.

This initial list showed the lack of a major group, civil society. A deliberate attempt was therefore made to identify suitable CSOs through an Internet search and a review of civil society databases. While rich in potential contacts, the databases were of limited use, with information often out of date or incomplete, preventing identification of the relevant groups or individuals. This made it important to ask all stakeholders and contacts for recommendations, which yielded names of people and organizations which may otherwise have been overlooked.

Once the CSO networks became aware of MSG-Pharma, local and community-based groups whose activities covered only villages, or at most a district, contacted the group and asked to be part of it. Although of key importance in implementation of activities at local and community levels, such groups presented a problem in the initial stages of the MSG, as their geographical coverage is low and their numbers may be too large for effective coordinated action. This was solved by encouraging such groups to link with their parent associations, which MSG-Pharma then invited to join the coalition. The small organizations were included in the MSG database to receive regular communications and for future involvement as appropriate.

A lesson learned early in the process was the value of having an open mind in the identification of CSO partners and of seeing possibilities in organizations not necessarily directly involved in health or pharmaceutical issues. For example, one of the most committed members of the coalition was a teachers' association interested in the issue because it was relevant to members' roles as community leaders and in preparing their students in health issues.

While very advantageous, such a wide variety of membership can also raise problems. It was important to present the issues around pharmaceutical procurement in such a way that each stakeholder could see their interest being covered. For example, the teachers' group was able to see the availability of medicines as easing the workload for female carers in the family, therefore allowing better school attendance by girls. Likewise the regulatory authority saw the availability of medicines as important for its work, as this prevents the importation of substandard or illegal pharmaceuticals to cover deficits.

The final coalition that emerged contained 28 organizations: four from the public sector (MHSW Pharmaceutical Services Unit, PPRA, MSD, and TFDA), three universities, three professional associations, two NGOs, and 16 community-based organizations.

Identifying a Convener

The process of building consensus entails a number of key meetings and regular communication with stakeholders. The first step was to convene a broad-based stakeholder forum and present the findings from the desk review of the country context. This was followed by a brainstorming session in which each stakeholder outlined causes of failure in pharmaceutical procurement and supply chain management (PSM) from their perspective. Following discussion and agreement that the situation needed to be addressed, stakeholders gave a general commitment to participate in possible interventions. A steering group was then formed, with one member acting as the coordinator.

In Tanzania, the election of a convener was a drawn-out process requiring several meetings under the auspices of a steering committee. It was quickly realized that the convener had to be an individual in whom people had confidence. He or she also needed to belong to a reputable body which could become the organizational host or convener. A local university with a pharmacy school, St John's University of Tanzania, emerged as an acceptable host. The university was initially contracted to undertake the country study and desk review and, after the validation workshop, took the lead in transforming the group of stakeholders into the coalition. Consequently, the university representative was elected chairman of the coalition. The appointment of the university as convener provided the chairman with a stronger executive role—considered important in the formative period.

The selection of a convener needed to take into account several factors necessary for success. In Kenya, Transparency International (TI Kenya) convened a meeting of potential members. Eventually, when FoTAPP was formally established, TI Kenya was nominated as convener by vote. The FoTAPP Memorandum of Understanding (MoU) now provides a mechanism for the appointment of a convener.

Broad lessons learned in identifying a convener include the following:

- People active in the coalition, such as steering committee members or the convener, are not necessarily the top decision makers in their respective organizations. For example, the convener was from the pharmacy school, but decisions were made by the vice-chancellor, as head of the university. Likewise, the representative from MHSW would need to report to the permanent secretary[4] or the minister. It was therefore necessary to inform and convince senior MHSW officials of the importance of the exercise, so that they supported any agreed activities and the involvement of their representative on the committee or as convener. In Tanzania, senior-level buy-in was achieved by forming teams to pay courtesy visits to heads of member organizations. Where possible, personal links were used to open doors to these senior officials.
- Convening also involves time and some financial commitment, which can present a challenge, especially for smaller organizations. This investment can

only be assured if an organization sees that the work of the coalition will in the long run support or promote its objectives. For the university, the possibility of becoming a center of excellence in pharmaceutical procurement was sufficient incentive.

• It is important to keep stakeholders informed to retain their interest and build ownership of the coalition. The convener must have the skills and facilities for effective communication, for example, by phone, email, or travel for face-to-face meetings. Support systems such as an office with Internet access and administrative back-up are also necessary.

Clarifying Responsibilities

In a multistakeholder group, each member must be and feel responsible for some aspect of the collaboration. A clear understanding of roles and responsibilities is essential in such a diverse group. It was therefore necessary for MSG-Pharma to define clearly the role of the convener, the steering committee, and other stakeholders. Through a consultative process of meetings and email interactions, terms of reference for the convener and the steering committee were developed.

An interim leadership made up of steering committee members was appointed at a members' meeting. In selecting steering committee personnel, it was important to consider representation of different stakeholder groups, as well as key skills and knowledge required on the committee. Pharmaceutical, financial, and legal expertise needed to be available within the team. It was also important to discuss in advance what commitments in terms of time, finance, or other resources were required. An organization's history of participation in previous meetings was considered as an indicator of whether its representative would be available for steering committee activities.

The leadership was tasked with holding meetings to discuss the most suitable structure and mandate for the coalition. It reviewed the structures of similar coalitions, such as FoTAPP in Kenya, and drafted organizational tools. These included the MSG-Pharma profile, which served as an introduction to external parties, as well as an MoU between members and the rules of engagement (referred to as the Code of Conduct). With the competing interests and divergent views inherent in multistakeholder groups, an understanding of how members would work together was needed. In Tanzania, MSG members prepared the Code of Conduct (see appendix D) to address issues such as barriers to consensus building, disruptive behavior, conflict, and negotiating win-win deals. The Code of Conduct specified that members would engage in active listening, respect the views of other members, disagree without being disagreeable, and strive for the greatest possible degree of transparency. A working draft of the code was developed using examples from other organizations, comprehensive enough to cover the group's diverse interests, and requirements. These documents were written in simple language that would not be intimidating and yet would convey to all members what was expected of them.

MeTA Uganda also has a set of internal rules to help guide members in these areas. The challenges it encountered were mainly those of process, including the following:

- Variable participation
- Voluntary governance, with no direct incentives
- Mistaken external perceptions—for example, CSOs initially perceived MeTA Uganda as a funding organization
- Government sensitivity that disclosure of public sector information should be met with reciprocal benefit from the West. This required the packaging of information, so that appropriate material was provided to suitable audiences who would use it to help the coalition's cause, for example, through advocacy
- Much information needed by MeTA for its work was still in hard copy or simple Excel sheets, due to the lack of automation in various government departments
- In some instances the linkage between disclosure and evidence for policy change was not clear, as the pilot phase was deemed too short for meaningful disclosure and reforms were anticipated in the medium to long term
- Apprehension, owing to a lack of clarity at the beginning, over what value some stakeholders would add to the process. It was therefore important to gain a shared understanding of different stakeholders' competencies and to train the coalition in multistakeholder processes. This was achieved through:
  - A MeTA "champion"—in this case, the MoH Principal Pharmacist, who worked closely with the local consultant to secure buy-in from the ministry and ensure that a coordinator was hired. This provided an enabling environment for the coalition's launch.
  - The availability of funding for workplan activities
  - Cooperation from the government on the reform agenda
  - A coordinator to facilitate discussions at council meetings and between stakeholders
  - Oversight, capacity building, and technical expertise from the international MeTA Secretariat
  - A legal framework within which to operate, pertaining to Uganda's health care provision and enshrining accountability in the country's constitution.

Developing Local Capacity

It was also important to create materials that each stakeholder could understand, such as information about the availability of medicines. This meant not only using an appropriate language—English or a local dialect—but also making technical information understandable to lay people. To enable this, workshops were organized on basic procurement and supply chain management (PSM) principles, tailored to civil society representatives. At a preliminary workshop, the coalition in Tanzania identified CSOs to be trained, selecting those likely to play a big role in monitoring, advocacy, and training other CSO leaders. Facilitators from Kenya, Tanzania, and Uganda conducted the training. Subsequently, the coalition groups from all three countries developed a "Training of Trainers" manual on PSM, based on the gaps in civil society capacity previously identified. The manual was designed to demystify PSM and equip CSOs with skills and competencies to monitor service providers and hold them accountable. It was also intended to provide a valuable learning resource with vital technical information which could help CSOs better engage with practitioners in the public and private spheres.

With potential stakeholders identified and trained, the next question was how MSG members would coordinate themselves.

Making the Coalition Work

To give the coalition the joint goals that would hold it together, the first activity was to develop and agree shared mission and vision statements. These were to be included in a broad-based profile of the coalition that would be used to introduce it to external organizations. A small task force was created to review the multistakeholder philosophy in the context of country conditions and expected activities, and develop the mission and vision statements. These statements were later presented to a full meeting of MSG-Pharma for approval.

This approach contrasts with that taken in Uganda, where MeTA Uganda adopted a set of guiding principles, rather than mission and vision statements. These principles were formulated by the International MeTA Secretariat and embraced by all stakeholders:

- Governments are responsible for providing access to health care, including access to essential medicines.
- Stronger and more transparent systems and improved supply chain management will increase access to medicines.
- Increased equitable access to medicines improves health and enables other human development objectives to be achieved.
- Improved information about medicines can fuel public debate and provide a basis for better policy.
- A multistakeholder approach that involves all sectors—private, public, and civil society—will lead to greater accountability by all.

In Uganda, trust was built over time as the different stakeholders engaged with a common purpose and contributed their specific competencies and expertise. It was understood that despite their various perspectives, all were working toward a common goal and that this could be done synergistically. The World Bank, in the role of facilitator, sponsored a capacity-building event in multistakeholder processes, which was instrumental in helping build trust. This workshop gave participants an understanding of the internal dynamics of complex social and organizational networks by explaining systems theory and its application to the coalition. Through coordination sessions and meetings of the secretariat to discuss implementation of the workplan, a shared vision and mission to increase access to medicines were developed. Different views on how best to achieve this were discussed until members reached consensus through a majority vote (one vote per member). The coalition's approach was subsequently reviewed regularly to ensure the continuing relevance of its actions.

Multistakeholder groups are instruments of the communities in which they operate. Their visibility is therefore important in gaining community attention. In Tanzania, a high-profile launch was needed to announce the birth of the coalition and capture the notice of the public. The launch was officiated by the chairperson of the Parliamentary Committee for Social Services, a figure with a national profile, in the presence of each coalition member, health sector dignitaries, and the national media. A centerpiece of the launch was the signing by all members of the MoU to establish the coalition.

Members decided to prioritize the monitoring of procurement and stocks of medicines, in response to the government reform agenda of decentralizing and strengthening service delivery at LGA level. Through stakeholder analysis they identified key coalition players (such as PPRA and MSD), as well as partners outside the coalition (such as officials at the district level where monitoring was to take place) to undertake different roles during the monitoring exercise.

The monitoring was to involve three major groups: pharmacists, procurement officers, and civil society members. In order to make sure there was common understanding of the task and procedure, and to build technical capacity, MSG-Pharma held training and debriefing workshops on contract monitoring, attended by civil society monitors, district officials, and government bodies such as MHSW, MSD, and PPRA.

Collaboration between coalition members required a mechanism for sharing information and providing feedback, for example, on draft documents. A system was agreed, including responding to emails or giving feedback within a specified time, attending planned meetings, or confirming referrals and contacts details. To ensure open lines of communication, contact information was kept by the convener and made available to all MSG members. A group mailing system ensured communications reached every member.

Owing to the differing strengths of MSG members in terms of influence, resources, and knowledge, there was a need to ensure every voice was heard. This was addressed by giving each category of stakeholder representation on the steering committee or any subcommittee. Group members also made sure stakeholder capabilities were fully leveraged by allocating tasks according to strengths. For example, the PPRA was tasked with providing samples of contract monitoring tools which could be adapted for use in the MSG-Pharma study to assess pharmaceutical procurement practices at district level, with a focus on compliance with the Public Procurement Act. Academic institutions led in the development of tools and resource materials, government members helped obtain consent for the study from district authorities, and civil society led in monitoring. Every member was asked to make use of their contacts whenever possible so that relationships could be leveraged within and beyond the coalition.

This contrasts with the experiences of MeTA Uganda, whose members soon realized they had an uneven playing field. It had been envisaged that information asymmetry could be tackled through training for CSOs, coordination meetings with rotating cochairs and a separate secretariat able to follow up various stakeholders, who had a platform on which to present their issues. Each member's available resources were made known publically. Through Information and Communications Technology (ICT) platforms, discussions were often initiated online, and recommendations ended up in council meetings for decisions to be taken. In order to leverage stakeholders' respective strengths, there was representation of each member at council and secretariat level.

With the execution of the MeTA Uganda workplan, training workshops on multistakeholder coalitions, and expansion of the MeTA Uganda agenda (to include transparency and accountability in public pharmaceutical supply chain systems), there was consensus that some important stakeholders were not represented on the council. These missing voices were eventually co-opted, including the Public Procurement and Disposal Authority, the media, and academia. The work on monitoring the medicine supply chain system was also integrated into the broader MeTA Uganda agenda during the expansion phase, as it sought to diversify its resource base and enlist more partners for sustainability.

Lessons Learned

Understand the Reform Agenda

A multistakeholder coalition is a social tool used to enhance a reform agenda. It draws its strength from its members, who have vested interests in particular reforms. For this reason, the reform agenda must be well articulated and all members must have a similar understanding of prevailing issues. A detailed study and report—as carried out in Tanzania—can help define relevant issues for all stakeholders.

Such an initial study or desk review is a situational analysis, not focused on a particular agenda, but aimed at helping members determine which agenda they should focus on. The study must therefore be broad based and detailed, reflecting familiarity with the sector under review.

In some cases, the reform agenda might have been set by parties external to a coalition, as was the case for groups in the mining and construction sectors in Tanzania. Even under such circumstances, a detailed study of the forces underlying the decision to form a coalition is necessary. Without this, members might differ in their understanding of the issues addressed by the coalition. Situational analyses help define the terms of reference for an MSG.

It is also important to remember that reform is fluid. A situation described in a particular review will at some stage be surpassed by events and become irrelevant. It is essential to undertake frequent surveys after a coalition has been formed—as carried out by MeTA Uganda and FoTAPP in Kenya—in order to determine whether any issues have evolved. The aim of such studies is similar to the initial study conducted in Tanzania—to understand the prevailing reform agenda in order to decide whether to continue or alter a course of action.

Consult Stakeholders Appropriately

For an MSG to position itself correctly and attract credible members, an extensive stakeholder consultation must be undertaken before the group's establishment. In Tanzania, health care reforms targeted service delivery at local authority level, but stakeholders interested in the multistakeholder process came from national institutions helping to guide the agenda (for example, the Program Support Unit and MSD) or monitor its implementation (for example, PPRA). However, before these key stakeholders were identified, a very wide net was cast, with the initial process including private sector health providers, business people, professional associations, and academia. These potential stakeholders subsequently dropped off when the group focused on activities not immediately central to their interests.

The absence of CSOs in the consultation process was notable and was due to the fact that none were active in the area of reform at the time. Under normal circumstances, relevant CSOs would be identified in the desk review and consequently invited to consultation meetings. Depending on context, there are widely varied definitions of which organizations constitute civil society, but it is important that such definitions remain the prerogative of individual coalitions. The broadest definition of civil society as given by NGO associations in Tanzania includes cooperatives, faith-based organizations, community-based organizations, and informal grassroots organizations. The key to a particular definition adopted by a coalition must be to include those organizations that are not represented among its membership in other ways. For example, in Tanzania, faith-based organizations and professional societies were not included in the definition of civil society, and the term was used to describe community-based organizations only.

Allow Flexible and Constructive Stakeholder Engagement

The activities to be monitored by an MSG may be either preconceived (as in Tanzania's mining sector coalition, whose membership was determined by the government) or developed in the process of setting up the coalition. The latter was the case for MSG-Pharma, which started with over 60 stakeholders, although only 24 signed the final MoU to launch the coalition. This demonstrates a stakeholder attrition rate that is unavoidable—as well as healthy.

MSGs driven by voluntary participation are the most prone to membership attrition, due to the variety of interests in the MSG's particular agenda. A common purpose alone is not sufficient to maintain interest throughout the lifecycle of the coalition. It is important to expect attrition and to make provision for members to leave or return, depending on the agenda advanced by the coalition at any particular moment. Allowing members to come and go is healthy for a voluntary organization, providing for the presence at any one time of members with the high interest and expectations necessary to channel the coalition's energy towards achieving its objectives. While a sizeable membership is an asset, a large number of participants can also bog down deliberations and decision making.

An MSG should not wait for the group to grow in number before starting its activities, but should start with the few members who are committed. Even just two or three people ready to participate should be encouraged to start taking action. Others who are lukewarm will join when they begin to see results. To this end, the group should start with something easily achievable—gathering the "low-hanging fruit".

It is important to be aware that the existence of a coalition may raise expectations, and to prepare in advance for how to prevent or handle these. For example, in Tanzania, MSG-Pharma trained CSOs in the pilot region to monitor. However, after carrying out work using their new skills, they did not receive the report on the outcomes as soon as they had expected, and asked repeatedly why the dissemination of the final report was delayed. Regular communication to inform them about progress was necessary. An MSG should also know how to communicate sensitive information, especially if it is negative about a stakeholder. The most effective way of working is not "tell and shame" but "show and help", so that stakeholders are supported to improve their performance or approach, rather than condemned.

Choose the Most Appropriate Type of Coalition
The three coalitions working in East Africa's pharmaceutical sector have different approaches with regard to stakeholder collaboration. In Tanzania and Kenya, members opted for loose coalitions—almost networks—with no legal mandate. These coalitions are hosted by conveners, who provide secretarial and legal capacity. Such arrangements relieve members of the legal obligation of running a coalition, in favor of voluntary obligations. On the contrary, in Uganda, a secretariat was established with a full-time coordinator charged with the day-to-day administration of MeTA Uganda. This was possible due to financial support from donors—which also necessitated the creation of a legal body for accountability purposes. Both arrangements have proved successful, but both require a champion (an influential person who advocates on behalf of the group) to maintain momentum when the process seems to be stalling. Such a champion sustains the interest of members and promotes the objectives of the coalition at a very high level.

Cement Ways of Working through Formal Documentation
MSG-Pharma and FoTAPP have MoUs, while MeTA Uganda has a memorandum of association. These two documents have different implications. Generally,

MoUs are not legally binding, but they carry a degree of importance and mutual respect, stronger than a gentlemen's agreement. They are used to embody the understanding of the parties in principle without creating any right or obligation of binding nature enforceable by a court of competent jurisdiction, allowing more room for members to come and go as they see fit. Conversely, memoranda of association are guided by law, requiring formal admission and greater commitment. However, both forms have worked well so far.

Select the Right Convener

A good MoU or memorandum of association is important for laying down the framework for collaboration (see box 2.2). However, this framework will not be successful if the convener is weak or not wholly convinced of his or her role or the coalition's mission and vision. A convener must:

- Be knowledgeable of the reform agenda addressed by the coalition
- Have adequate resources to carry out the role
- Have strong connections within the sector
- Be strongly committed to the coalition's vision.

A convener can be an individual or an institution. For a coalition with a full-time secretariat arising from a memorandum of association, the convener would most likely be an individual employed in that capacity. In such cases, the recruitment process must be technically sound in order to select a candidate of suitable caliber. Remuneration may be significant in obtaining such an individual, so the coalition must consider its resources before taking this approach.

Box 2.2 Essential Elements of an MoU for a Multistakeholder Group

Regardless of an MoU's simplicity, it must address several key areas:

- The coalition's objectives
- Membership criteria and obligations
- Provisions for a code of conduct (see box 2.3) or internal rules
- Management structure and election of a chairperson and steering committee members
- Role of convener
- Ownership of property, products, and publications
- Defining and providing for declaration of conflicts of interest
- Limiting members' liability
- Resolution of disputes
- Duration and terms of the MoU
- How to amend or dissolve the MoU.

Box 2.3 What Should a Code of Conduct Cover?

A Code of Conduct addresses ethical and moral issues relating to the terms of association. It can be very helpful in enabling all voices in a coalition to be heard. Basic issues that should be addressed include the following:

- Prevention of discrimination
- Observance of the law
- Truth and honesty
- Mutual respect between all members
- Being a model of transparency and accountability
- Equality in participation
- Gender equality
- Joint accountability
- No political affiliations
- Self-respect and self-confidence
- Service to the public
- Unity and focus on the coalition's objectives
- Using information collected by the coalition for intended purposes only
- Declaration of conflicts of interest.

An institutional convener will appoint one of its employees to perform the role. The institution must be a member of the coalition and must have adequate resources to support the coalition in emergencies. As coalitions can have very fluid membership, the institution that hosts the secretariat must be among the most strongly committed members.

Where the coalition is based on an MoU, the host organization will be required to provide the legal front for the coalition. In most cases, this will require support from the organization's top management and agreement in writing. An exchange of commitment letters may be necessary to guarantee this obligation. Where possible, relationships should be allowed to develop gradually, to provide members with time to get to know each other and assess the situation.

It is important to understand that by agreeing to be under the legal umbrella of the host institution, the coalition will automatically be subject to that organization's financial controls, as required by various laws. For example, legislation relating to tax payment will not distinguish between payments made for the coalition and those of the host organization. Such consequences must be understood and acknowledged before the final agreement is reached.

The person appointed by the host organization to lead the coalition secretariat must be committed, of high integrity and widely respected in the sector. In most cases this individual would be the institution's representative in the coalition and would be well known to other members. If the appointee is not a representative in the coalition, its members should define the candidate's desirable qualifications and characteristics before the appointment by the host association. The convener will be required to work very closely with the coalition leadership, so it must be consulted before a candidate is formally appointed.

Define and Focus on Priorities

It is important to realize that results are what will give the coalition a profile and sustain its existence. Understanding the reform agenda will help the coalition choose which issues to address. However, this alone will not produce results. The coalition needs to build financial and human resource capacity and needs specific strategies to mobilize such resources. This requires strong management skills. The coalition should adopt the latest planning and monitoring techniques—for example, management by results—to prepare, adopt, and implement action plans. "Quick wins"—activities that bring quick results in a short time—are particularly important in building confidence and gaining visibility.

Finances are crucial, but a coalition should also seek other types of support, such as political will. Tanzania's MSG-Pharma enjoyed the support of the Dodoma regional authorities, which opened doors in the health facilities being monitored. For sustainability, a coalition must continuously seek to diversify its resource base and partnerships, yet for credibility it must also maintain its independence. For this reason, MeTA Uganda declined government funding at the end of the pilot phase. An independent stance, anchored in the coalition's objectives, must be maintained throughout its duration.

Notes

1. Health sector strengthening programs have also been taking place in Kenya and Uganda.

2. Tanzania World Bank Project Appraisal Document (2011): The sector-wide approach (SWAP) was initiated in 1999 in the health sector in Tanzania. It provides the framework for collaboration among the stakeholders, MHSW, regional administration and local government departments, the Ministry of Finance, civil society, the private sector, and development partners. It coordinates financing, planning, and monitoring mechanisms and aims at creating synergies while reducing transaction costs. Central in the SWAP is the implementation of health policies and the HSSP.

3. In 2010, the World Bank Institute (WBI) conducted rapid country assessments to determine governance issues in pharmaceutical procurement in Tanzania, Uganda, and Kenya through four activities: a desk review, consultations with key informants, a benchmarking assessment of each country's medicine procurement agency, and an in-country validation meeting.

4. Permanent secretaries are the nonpolitical civil service heads of government departments, who generally hold their position for a number of years at a ministry, as distinct from the changing political ministers of state to whom they report and provide advice.

CHAPTER 3

Growing a Strong Trunk
Nourishing and Sustaining the Coalition Tree

Debra Gichio, Teresa Omondi, and Abel Nyakiongora

Introduction

Coalitions involve joint action by their members toward the sustainable attainment of shared goals. Nourishing and strengthening relations between these members require different strategies and continuous responding to each organization's needs, according to their purpose for being in the coalition. This chapter describes the experience of Kenyan stakeholders in sustaining the Forum for Transparency and Accountability in Pharmaceutical Procurement (FoTAPP), a coalition whose main objective is to monitor the procurement of pharmaceuticals in the country, in order to improve citizens' access to essential medicines.

The chapter focuses on key lessons learned in sustaining multistakeholder coalitions. Once a coalition has been set up—its mission and vision established, stakeholders mobilized, rules of engagement drawn, and a set of activities agreed—there is a need to invest in efforts that strengthen it and provide a platform for implementing transformative programs. Without interventions that build trust and solidify stakeholder commitment, maintaining momentum will be difficult.

The chapter also provides insights into the approaches employed by FoTAPP in order to sustain the interest and commitment of key stakeholders. It presents a brief description of the Kenyan context in relation to the pharmaceutical sector, highlighting challenges in the sector and the importance of a multistakeholder coalition amid other reform platforms. Strategies key to making a coalition sustainable are outlined, including the following:

- Mobilizing resources effectively (both financial and in terms of members' time)
- Harnessing members' expertise, contacts, and access to information
- Pegging coalition activities onto members' existing activities

- Creating a leadership structure that provides effective oversight of activities, gives guidance, neutralizes tensions, and overcomes stalemates
- Nominating member organizations as project champions, according to their expertise
- Providing platforms for constructive dialogue
- Ensuring transparency in the use of coalition funds and project status
- Creating ownership among members, for example, by equal involvement in decision making
- Giving members strong incentives, for example, capacity building, networking
- Acknowledging member's contributions and celebrating results and achievements.

FoTAPP's experience reveals vital lessons for developing and nurturing successful coalitions, as outlined in box 3.1.

Kenya Country Context

Overview of Pharmaceutical Sector

In its latest census (2008–09) (Kenya Demographic and Health Survey 2010), Kenya had a population of 39.4 million. With an estimated percentage increase of 2.8 per year, the country is estimated in 2014 to have over 40 million people. The demand for medicines in the domestic market is driven by a number of related factors, such as disease incidence and type (for example, human immunodeficiency virus [HIV] and acquired immune deficiency syndrome [AIDS], malaria, tuberculosis), procurement and distribution, exports, and health insurance.

Box 3.1 Key Lessons in the Establishment of a Multistakeholder Group: Kenya

1. Build relationships proactively within the coalition—Ensure strong leadership that can nurture relationships, balance each member's needs, and constantly direct members toward the coalition's common mission.
2. Ensure members' organizational commitment at the highest level—This helps gain quick approval of the coalition's decisions, strengthens its credibility, and ensures members remain engaged in coalition work when an individual representative leaves a member organization.
3. Have a clear coalition agenda—Ensure all members understand the coalition's purpose and scope, to prevent individual organizations introducing their own agendas.
4. Ensure sustainable financial resources—The coalition must remain continuously mindful of the need to be sustainable, for example, engaging support from its target audience for an initiative.
5. Emphasize the common goal—This will help the coalition through potentially challenging situations, for example, if it is required to monitor a member's performance.

Kenya has a decentralized system of governance created by the Constitution of 2010. The new structure comprises two levels of government: 47 county administrations and the national government. The public delivery system for health care is organized in a conventional pyramid structure, with dispensaries providing first-level care, health centers and subcounty hospitals at the next level, followed by county hospitals. At the apex of the pyramid are two referral hospitals, the Moi Teaching and Referral Hospital in Eldoret and the Kenyatta National Hospital in Nairobi. These referral hospitals are the only health facilities that remain under the direct supervision of the national Ministry of Health. Public health facilities account for 48 percent of all health facilities in the country, while those owned by faith-based organizations and nongovernmental organizations (NGOs) account for 14 percent, and 38 percent are privately owned.

Kenya is currently the largest producer of pharmaceutical products in the Common Market for Eastern and Southern Africa (COMESA), supplying about 50 percent of the region's market (KAM Pharmaceutical & Medical Equipment Sector 2014). However, the pharmaceutical sector is a complex one, involving many different players, including manufacturers, national regulators, government ministries, wholesalers, distributors, retailers, and consumers. Kenya has increasingly realized that to create the environment in which the pharmaceutical industry can flourish requires concerted action across these stakeholders. Only then can the sector realize its full potential as an asset to economic and social development.

The Procurement and Distribution of Medicines

In Kenya, the supply of pharmaceuticals to public health facilities is the preserve of the Kenya Medical Supplies Agency (KEMSA). By law, KEMSA is responsible for procurement, warehousing and distribution of medicines and medical supplies to such facilities across the country. This near-monopolistic arrangement has experienced challenges that affect access to medicines and medical supplies. A multistakeholder coalition, FoTAPP, was set up to focus on transparency in pharmaceutical procurement as one of the means by which access to medicines and medical supplies could be improved.

It has been estimated that KEMSA's purchases constitute 30 percent of all prescription drugs in the Kenyan market. The pharmaceutical distribution system in Kenya can be classified into public (government), NGO, and private channels. Public sector procurement in Kenya is both centralized and decentralized, both options managed by KEMSA. KEMSA also procures medicines for some donor partners.

Another bulk procurer of medicines is the Mission for Essential Drugs and Supplies (MEDS), a not-for-profit organization which purchases medical items for faith-based organizations (FBOs) and some donors. Private sector procurement and distribution is handled by various pharmacies and private health facilities.

Accelerating Health Reforms through Collective Action • http://dx.doi.org/10.1596/978-1-4648-0287-4

Legal Framework

The main legislation for control of the pharmaceutical sector in Kenya is the Pharmacy and Poisons Act, Cap 244. Its main purpose is to regulate the profession of pharmacy and to control the manufacturing, trade, and distribution of pharmaceutical products.

The recently enacted Kenya Medical Supplies Agency Act, 2013, provided autonomy to KEMSA to procure, warehouse, and distribute medicines, medical supplies for prescribed public health programs, and the national strategic stock reserve. KEMSA is equally mandated to support county governments to establish and maintain appropriate supply chain systems for medicines and medical supplies.

Other relevant laws include the following:

- Industrial Property Act, 2001. Popularly known as the "Patent Act", this provides for the promotion of innovation, to facilitate the acquisition of technology by granting and regulating patents, utility models, inventions, and industrial designs. Kenya acceded to the Trade-Related Intellectual Property Services (TRIPS) agreement by enacting this legislation in 2001.
- Anti-Counterfeit Act, December 2008. This prohibits trade in counterfeit goods, including pharmaceuticals.
- Kenya Public Procurement and Disposal Act, 2005. This establishes the procedures for public procurement.

Pharmaceutical Regulation and Governance

The regulatory authority for Kenya's pharmaceutical sector is the Pharmacy and Poisons Board , established by law under the Pharmacy and Poisons Act, Cap 244. The board regulates the practice of pharmacy and the manufacture and trade of medicines and poisons. The National Quality Control Laboratory was established as the technical arm of the board, to provide for the examination and testing of drugs and to ensure quality control.

Organizations governing the sector include the following:

- Federation of Kenya Pharmaceutical Manufacturers (FKPM)
- Kenya Association of Pharmaceutical Industry (KAPI)
- Kenya Association of Manufacturers (KAM)
- Kenya Private Sector Alliance (KEPSA)
- Kenya Health Federation (KHF)
- Pharmaceutical Society of Kenya (PSK)
- Various Civil Society Organizations (CSOs) working in the health sector and on governance. (FoTAPP has a membership of 40 CSOs interested in the procurement and supply of pharmaceutical and nonpharmaceutical products.)

The Pharmaceutical Sector and the Reform Agenda

Access to health care and the availability and affordability of medicines are key health issues for the poor in Kenya. A study by the Ministry of Health supported by the World Health Organization (WHO), Health Action International-Africa (HAI-A), and HAI-A partners in Kenya (Medicine Prices in Kenya 2005) highlighted factors that contributed to high and variable prices for medicines and identified strategies and policies to improve their affordability.

Factors inhibiting access include insufficient health financing, deficiencies in human resources, poor physical infrastructure, stock-outs of basic essential medicines, and deficiencies in pharmaceutical commodity supply and management. In 2012, FoTAPP carried out a citizen satisfaction survey in which staff at participating facilities expressed dissatisfaction with the timeliness of supplies, the use of Information and Communications Technology (ICT) for effective tracking and evaluation, and the handling of emergency supplies. Other weaknesses had been reported in a KEMSA Customer Satisfaction Report of 2011, including complaint handling procedures, poor information sharing, inefficient drug redistribution, poor problem solving, poor timeliness of supplies, and stock-outs.

Concerted efforts to approach pharmaceutical challenges in Kenya are as old as the industry itself. For example, stakeholders are unified with regard to the scourge of counterfeit drugs, which cause huge health problems and threaten legitimate manufacturers, who effectively have to compete with substandard products. The voice of civil society working in the health sector was loud in differentiating counterfeit drugs from generic drugs, believed to be accessible and affordable to the majority, ultimately saving lives.

The legal standard for access to health care is set out by Article 43 of Kenya's Constitution, which provides that every individual has the right to the highest attainable standard of health, including the right to health care services. Public participation is key in attaining this right. Health sector stakeholders (public, private, and civil society) are fully aware that reform in the sector needs to tackle barriers to access in order to meet the constitutional standard. However, these stakeholders need to sit around one table, each bringing their different expertise to strengthen governance in pharmaceutical procurement and supply management.

Rationale for Setting Up a Multistakeholder Coalition

At the time FoTAPP was established in 2011, Kenya was facing serious accountability challenges in public procurement. A lack of transparency was having significant consequences for public services, with 30 percent of the national revenue being lost in fraudulent procurement (Organization of Economic Cooperation and Development [OECD]). Meaningful citizen participation in decision making and the reform process was urgently needed. FoTAPP members unanimously agreed to concentrate on monitoring pharmaceutical procurement to ensure effective service delivery to citizens.

FoTAPP's multistakeholder approach includes a wide range of coalition members from various institutions and sectors. These members drive and sustain the coalition's agreed agenda—in FoTAPP's case, to enhance transparency and accountability in pharmaceutical procurement and supply chain management. The multistakeholder approach would allow the sharing of diverse expertise, knowledge, and experience between members, thereby improving their capacities. Transparency International Kenya (TI Kenya) was selected as the coalition convener.

Moving the Reform Agenda Forward

The multistakeholder approach drove the reform agenda by identifying existing gaps in the pharmaceutical supply chain and developing appropriate interventions in response. Working in coalition has improved stakeholders' knowledge and understanding of pharmaceutical procurement, and enhanced monitoring of procurement and supply chain management (PSM) in the sector. Key activities included the development of relevant tools to enable standardized monitoring. Coalition members are able to hold each other accountable for any problems that arise, not necessarily casting blame but openly discussing concerns through a participatory approach and coming up with sustainable solutions.

The development and application of monitoring tools provided opportunities for joint investment of resources—time, staff, and finances—due to shared objectives among members of the coalition. One such intervention under FoTAPP is the mobile drug tracking system that sought to use a mobile application to support citizens in accessing information on the availability of medicines and on health facility drawing rights,[1] enabling group chat and registering patients' complaints. The coalition piloted tracking of pharmaceuticals using information technology, through the Mobile-phone Drug Tracking System (MDTS). This enables consumers to query the availability or otherwise of medicines along the supply chain. Their input was then integrated into the Logistics Management Information System (LMIS) unit in the Kenya Medical Supplies Authority (KEMSA).LMIS therefore enables facility staff to order products, track consignments, and give feedback using mobile applications. The system was developed in collaboration with KEMSA and now resides in the citizen feedback module in the E-Mobile platform that KEMSA is currently rolling out to Kenya's public health facilities.

Accountability is also top of the agenda for reforms in the public health sector. Through the Ministry of Health (which is represented in the coalition), FoTAPP has benefited from the findings and lessons learned from the pilot of the social accountability project implemented by the Ministry of Health with the support of the World Bank. Through this collaboration, the ministry has included CSOs and other partners in the development of a manual on social accountability. It has also constituted a technical working group to support the implementation of social accountability mechanisms. This engagement has resulted in the Draft National Health Policy for 2014 including components of social accountability.

With support from members such as KEMSA, the Ethics and Anti-Corruption Commission, the Public Procurement Oversight Authority (PPOA), and the Ministry of Health's Social Accountability Focal Point, the coalition carried out capacity building for Health Facility Management Committees in target facilities. This has contributed to an increase in knowledge on the functions of KEMSA and PPOA. It is important to note that when FoTAPP was established, the coalition's added value was not as evident as it is now. There were varying expectations among members—for example, members of civil society had to step back from their role as watchdog to government agencies, instead sitting together with them as partners. These government agencies viewed themselves as having the sole mandate to address public problems. This positioning had to be addressed at the establishment of the coalition, by emphasizing that the sole beneficiary of all efforts by the public and private sectors and civil society is the common citizen.

In addition, the coalition was established alongside other existing platforms, such as government partnerships with some development agencies, and bilateral partnerships with private sector players. Such platforms were successful to the extent of achieving their specific objectives, but were not able to address the larger issue of transparency and accountability in national pharmaceutical procurement. The coalition was, in some instances, viewed as a threat to these existing agreements, a duplication of efforts or even as simply a "busybody." Government agencies also had other expectations of civil society, expecting funding for government projects or strategic plans. This was far from the coalition's agenda. Initially, other coalition members expected that the government would see as obvious the benefits of working through a multistakeholder process. However, this was not the case. The coalition had to find middle ground from which to address the needs and expectations of each member by agreeing on a few priority areas of action beneficial to all members.

Nourishing and Sustaining the Coalition

The overall key to sustaining successful coalitions is the ability to have an impact on the target community, creating change and seeing results. This is achieved through the ability of the coalition to be flexible and adaptive to environmental changes. FoTAPP's central approach was to remain alert to any concerns arising among the membership and to remain continuously relevant to each member's reasons for joining the coalition. The leadership would rotate in order to provide new ideas and strategic direction. A coalition also has to deal with new members joining at different stages of development of the coalition and existing members leaving.

Other factors that helped the coalition toward sustainability included the following:

Accelerating Health Reforms through Collective Action • http://dx.doi.org/10.1596/978-1-4648-0287-4

Mobilizing Resources

Resource mobilization may be defined as a management process that involves identifying people who share the same values and taking steps to create relationships with them (Venture for Fund Raising 2000). Mobilizing resources goes beyond simply raising funds. It also comprises organizational development and management, communicating and prospecting, and relationship building (Venture for Fund Raising 2000). Resource mobilization is an important component in sustaining coalitions, as it provides nourishment for growth, and solidifies relationships and collaborations.

Mobilizing resources for a coalition not only involves financial contributions but also includes nonmonetary resources such as time, expertise, and facilitation of logistics. For instance, coalition members sacrifice time in participating in coalition initiatives, communicating and coordinating, and sharing experiences. Members also contribute expertise, including professional advice, research, and the development of documents. Contribution of resources also includes cofunding initiatives and covering expenses incurred in coalition work (such as travel costs, hosting meetings, and stationery) or other project funds. The soliciting of these contributions has been vital in ensuring that the coalition meetings and activities are undertaken with adequate contributions from members.

Like MSG-Pharma in Tanzania, FoTAPP at its initiation received seed funding and technical support from the World Bank Institute. This aimed at bringing together partners and introducing the concept of the multistakeholder approach. The funds also supported the formulation of governance structures, the development of work plans, and resources to implement activities once the coalition was mobilized. Although it lacked the substantial funding from the UK's Department for International Development (DFID) enjoyed by the Medicines Transparency Alliance (MeTA) coalition in Uganda (which significantly reduced the task of resource mobilization for MeTA), FoTAPP and Tanzania's Multistakeholder Group on Pharmaceutical Procurement (MSG-Pharma) both managed to augment their resources to allow for successful implementation of their work plans, as discussed below.

Time as a Resource

To facilitate the implementation of various coalition activities, members of each coalition agreed on periodic meetings. FoTAPP agreed to meet every last Thursday of the month for at least three hours, and equivalent to approximately US$240 in consultant's fees.[2] Tanzania and Uganda coalitions met every two months. These scheduled times did not preclude the convener from calling for ad hoc meetings according to need, as was the case during the formative stage of the coalition.

The meetings were aimed at discussing the progress of the coalition, following up on previously agreed actions, providing new ideas, and distributing responsibilities for action. Prior to these meetings there were various e-mail discussions over thematic areas and decision making over key issues. Time allocated to participate in such discussions was acknowledged as a key resource, since each member organization contributed staff time[3] to do so.

Expertise

The coalition comprised various institutions that contributed professionals in law, health, media and communication, political science, supply chain management, human resource management, research, environmentalism, and statistics, among others. All these individuals contributed specialist opinions on issues pertaining to their expertise, which would otherwise have been paid for. For instance, in Kenya, legal opinion would on average cost $500 per pronouncement. This expense was saved by having lawyers on board who provided this advice at no cost. As a result, FoTAPP was able to draft various tools and reports at minimal cost by harnessing the expertise of coalition members and eliminating the need for consultants. Such expertise was similarly used to train members for free.

Accessing research documentation was equally made easy and faster, saving time and funds. All three countries had government partners in the coalition, which enabled prompt access to relevant unpublished government documents. The same applied to development partners and specialized civil society and private sector members.

Financial Resources

Finances were crucial to the success of the coalition work. Seed funds were needed to initiate the first meetings, sell the idea to stakeholders, and establish strong governance systems. Where finances are not directly given for coalition activities, a coalition has to leverage existing initiatives that are already funded.

FoTAPP identified several methods for obtaining funds:

- *Cofunding by stakeholders*—Coalition partners identified budget lines in their ongoing activities to contribute to the coalition's activities. For example, the use of data to enhance transparency and accountability in the health sector is a key strategic area for the National Taxpayers Association (NTA),[4] one of the coalition members. NTA therefore contributed money from its project funds to support data collection for the baseline health sector survey that would guide the work of the coalition.
- *Proposals to development partners*—FoTAPP successfully bid for funding from the World Bank Civil Society Fund, receiving US$100,000 to collect data to evaluate citizen satisfaction with health service delivery (among other activities). As the coalition convener, Transparency International Kenya (TI Kenya) led in drafting the proposal and had three other organizations sign it. Applying for the funds as a coalition increased the chances of winning funding, because the coalition was able to take advantage of the credibility of its member organizations with a proven track record in a particular area of focus.
- *Riding on stakeholder project activities*—Coalition members pegged some of their activities on fellow member organizations' activities. Most frequent was

Accelerating Health Reforms through Collective Action • http://dx.doi.org/10.1596/978-1-4648-0287-4

capacity building. For example, the Tanzania Public Procurement and Regulatory Authority (PPRA) had funds to train stakeholders in contract monitoring. The Tanzania coalition benefited from this training fully funded by PPRA. In Kenya, TI Kenya had incorporated the health sector in its strategic plan and had previously launched the health sector report gauging the sector's levels of transparency and accountability. It had resources for enhancing transparency and accountability in public procurement using ICT solutions, so it contributed toward the Mobile Drug Tracking System steered by the coalition.

- *Leveraging relationships*—The coalition has used its portfolio of members and their expertise to profile its members and attract funding by including the profiles in proposal documents and highlighting the relationships that exist with the target institution. It has also developed funding proposals that leverage its partnerships with members to highlight its broad range of strengths and skills.

An example is the pilot of the Mobile Drug Tracking System[5]—the mobile phone-based technology that allows members of the public to query the availability of medicines in target facilities. The existing relationship between the coalition, the Ministry of Health, and KEMSA was a key factor in tipping the scale for the pilot, as the system could only be developed in collaboration with KEMSA (due to heavy reliance on its logistics management system) and the Ministry of Health (for the extraction of consumption data for public health facilities and physical access to the target facilities). This led to the system's being integrated into the KEMSA M-health platform (based on mobile technology).

The coalition also identified members as key partners in the implementation of a major funding proposal (discussed below). In order to secure funding for the citizen satisfaction survey, it developed proposals to facilitate the customization and validation of tools, highlighting the skills of key member organizations renowned in the field of social research.

Leadership

Leadership is a key component in the coordination of a coalition and in sustaining its momentum. A coalition's success requires mutual respect, with leadership as the cement that binds the support of others in the accomplishment of agreed objectives. Leaders organize, provide guidance, and can neutralize tensions and break stalemates in a coalition. There is therefore need for a clear governance structure that reinforces the legitimacy of the convener and defines the relationship between members.

Leadership Structures

Leadership of a coalition is determined by its members. In Kenya, the coalition has formalized its governance structure by concluding a Memorandum of Understanding (MoU) that guides the interactions of its members and assigns roles and responsibilities. The initial formation of the Kenya coalition was through the selection of key stakeholders working on issues related to access to medicines and health service delivery. This process was led by TI Kenya which convened the maiden meeting that brought together all the key actors in this area. This was followed by the nomination of the convener by consensus. The MoU defines the convener's leadership role to include the following:

- Coordinate representation of the coalition at various forums in and outside Kenya
- Oversee project implementation and provide feedback to the group, including appropriate reports. These functions would involve:
  - Supporting and undertaking resource mobilization efforts
  - Communicating on behalf of the coalition
  - Acting as custodian of joint funds and being accountable for expenditure
  - Acting as custodian of administrative documents including minutes, the MoU, and any other agreements
  - Overall coordination of the coalition, including updating the list of members.

The convener also has a role in moderating coalition meetings and giving general strategic direction. This clarity in roles has helped keep the coalition focused on agreed issues and facilitated smooth implementation of its projects, with active participation from members.

Identifying Champions

The coalition nominates member organizations to lead and act as champions in the implementation of components of its work. The selection process is based on the area of focus and the expertise of the institution, allowing different members the opportunity to take leading roles in various coalition activities. With support from the convener, lead organizations have responsibility for coordinating coalition members to ensure that a task is completed on time. Activities members have championed include:

- The development of social accountability and procurement assessment tools
- Data collection and report preparation
- Capacity building.

In some instances, lead organizations team up with the convener to function as a technical working group. Organizations with the required skills or expertise are selected by the coalition to support the implementation of specific activities. Members contribute in their area of expertise, enabling the coalition to benefit from their intellectual input at minimum or no cost. This has created a sense of ownership, as members have an intimate understanding of the coalition's project and tools.

In Uganda, the coalition succeeded in securing support from the Ministry of Health, as one of the institutions invited to its formative meetings. Through collaboration with the Ministry of Health representative (the principle pharmacist), MeTA Uganda has succeeded in embedding the coalition within the ministry's structures, giving it official recognition and allowing it to contribute to the reform agenda at key levels.

Using Effective Communication Strategies

To disseminate information, the coalition has employed various modes of communication, including social media, emails, meetings, as well as telephone calls, press, and publications for updates and reports. Most information and strategic documents are disseminated via email and discussed during meetings to ensure that even those members absent from meetings are able to access vital information, contribute to discussions, and remain engaged.

Facilitating Ongoing Dialogue and Promoting Transparency

Open, continual dialogue and the ongoing promotion of transparency are critical to a coalition's success in terms of recruitment and retention of its membership. Transparency and information sharing are at the core of good governance, promoting a sense of ownership, facilitating resource mobilization, sharing between members, and reducing resistance and opportunities for conflict. Stakeholder dialogue is generative; it discourages blaming for the past and creates a shared future.

- *Promoting dialogue*: The coalition was able retain and grow a membership beyond the initial members by facilitating platforms for constructive dialogue through the following:
  - Meetings: FoTAPP held monthly meetings, giving members an opportunity to contribute opinions and comment on various interventions. This meant that activities met little resistance and were actively supported by members.
  - Validation and review: Meetings for these purposes have served as key communication tools for collating feedback from members and other stakeholders. Periodic email updates and text messaging have been used to sustain interest and participation in coalition affairs.
  - Capacity building in communication: Coalition building requires tackling a complex array of challenges, one of which is getting the communication dimension right. Coalition members received training in effective communication and subsequently developed a communication strategy for the coalition. Allies and opponents of the reform agenda were identified through targeting strategies. A power analysis matrix was used to assess the relative power relationships among groups and individuals in favor or against the reform agenda to inform appropriate messaging. Uganda benefited from similar training. Its coalition has used its strategy to create broad-based understanding of the "crisis" of ineffective and wasteful health

service delivery at the facility level, and mobilized both supply-side and demand-side actors to address implementation hurdles identified through a citizen satisfaction survey, which covered more than 200 health facilities nationwide.

Through the coalition, members received social media training to equip them with skills to make use of new avenues of communication. In Uganda, the media practitioners were trained in proactive online reporting on access to medicines. This brought greater visibility and corresponding action on the availability of medicines, leading ultimately to the establishment of a medicines' monitoring unit in the office of the president.

- *Promoting transparency*: FoTAPP's MoU contains accountability clauses in the section on the roles of the convener, specifically stating that the convener is accountable for funds spent and should render accounts accordingly. The MoU ensures transparency is upheld by stating that the convener must allow members unfettered access to all coalition documents. Transparency is further enhanced through the circulation of reports, tools, and work plans, which are discussed and approved at monthly meetings. The coalition also promotes transparency and accountability by giving status reports on project implementation and financial accountability at each meeting.

Creating a Sense of Ownership

To sustain a successful relationship, members need to have a continuous sense of ownership of the coalition's processes and results, and to consider themselves as core partners. A sense of ownership is often more a psychological feeling than a legal position. This feeling of ownership is more critical in a coalition, giving contentment that each partner's opinion counts, creating trust, and reducing conflict.

The three country coalitions had different approaches to promoting a sense of ownership among members, including the following:

Purpose of the Coalition

The goal of the coalition has to largely fit into the agenda or strategic direction of each individual member. Among FoTAPP's teething problems was the need to agree on the coalition's key objectives and priority activities. After several consultations, members unanimously agreed to work on the overall supply chain of pharmaceuticals to ensure effective service delivery to citizens, rather than concentrating only on the procurement process. This harnessed a sense of belonging, contributing greatly to the retention and active engagement of members.

Governance and Selection of Leadership

A key component of ownership is involving members in the process of establishing the coalition's governance structure and leadership. The leader must be generally acceptable to all members in order to provide effective direction. The Ugandan coalition agreed on a governance structure that comprised a governing council and a secretariat. Tanzania has a steering committee and a convener, whereas Kenya has only a convener. The point here is to explore and decide which approach best works for a particular coalition; no one structure fits all.

Inclusion and Equal Participation of All Members

The three country coalitions achieved this through group emails to keep every member informed about coalition activities. As far as possible, roles were also assigned to each member. Without opportunities for service, members' interest may wane; they may also feel side-lined and neglected. The more members participate, the more integrated they become into the coalition.

Constant Communication

Regular updates by the conveners or secretariat keep members informed, and help members feel recognized and valued. To ensure that all members are catered for, a variety of communication methods may be used: texting, emails, and publications such as newsletters.

Decision-making Processes

Consensus building was the most common method used in arriving at favorable decisions. This avoided the division of members by creating a "winners versus losers" scenario, which is a major cause for the ineffectiveness or breakup of coalitions. Every member needs to feel equally that their ideas are incorporated in the coalition's processes.

Ownership of Benefits and Results

The word "we" has a magic effect in any coalition. Joint ownership of processes, benefits, and results—regardless of the amount of contribution by each member—creates a strong sense of ownership by the general membership. This includes taking collective responsibility for failures.

Providing the Right Incentives

Responsiveness to the Needs of Member Organizations

While coalitions do not offer monetary incentives for members, they maintain their interest by identifying activities relevant to members' organizational objectives, which in turn inspire contribution and participation. This was demonstrated by the ease with which all three coalitions were able to identify projects that could support their mandates. For example, Tanzania's Public Procurement Regulatory Authority (PPRA) was pleased to support a national monitoring group aimed at helping PPRA achieve its objectives. The authority fully funded the training of the Tanzania coalition in contract monitoring, as this would support its work. This arrangement was also a great incentive for PPRA to remain a member of the coalition. In Uganda, the Public Procurement and Disposal of Assets Authority (PPDA), an equally active member of MeTA Uganda, took a similar approach.

Capacity-Building Opportunities

Various training activities arise out of coalition building. Organizations focusing on training are attracted to coordinated groups of stakeholders, as they provide an opportunity to reach program implementers at the basic facility level, influence implementation, and ensure concrete actions take place, based on lessons learned. Development partners also provide learning opportunities by supporting members to attend forums that are beneficial to the work of the coalition. For example, the World Bank Institute (WBI) sponsored some members of the Kenya coalition to attend the fifth Latin American conference on Innovative Solutions toward the Achievement of the Right to Health, held in Brazil. Participants learned about Brazil's devolved system of health care governance. Given Kenya's own transition to a devolved governance system, the insights acquired through this knowledge exchange were shared with other FoTAPP members. The coalition has since developed various concepts for the implementation of best practices.

Generally, all the country coalition members benefited from WBI-facilitated training on topics such as the concept of a multistakeholder approach, understanding the basics of procurement, and effective communication. On successful completion, participants received certificates, which have boosted their career portfolios. Such capacity building opportunities remain a key incentive for membership.

Networking Opportunities

Coalition meetings provide space for members to share experiences, meet experts from different spheres, and interact beyond coalition activities. For example, coalition members helped the Procurement and Supply Chain Students Association of the University of Nairobi to finance its annual activities through a fundraising dinner.

Celebration and Acknowledgment of Shared Achievements

FoTAPP has achieved many successes, large and small, all facilitated by members' participation. An important part of maintaining momentum for the coalition has been members' celebration of these achievements. This begins by recognizing and acknowledging individual members for their intellectual contributions and any other form of support to the coalition. This is done internally during meetings through citing contributions made, or more formally through recognition in published materials. The coalition also holds events to share successes with stakeholders and acclaim the achievement of objectives. In Uganda, MeTA goes further by ensuring beneficiaries and stakeholders that participate in implementation are recognized and that the government makes commitments on identified issues.

At meetings, members are also able to publicize upcoming events that may require attendance by other members. This way, the respective institutions members belong to (in their regular jobs) can support each other and celebrate the achievements of fellow members. This has promoted cohesion within the coalition.

Challenges and Lessons Learned

Working in coalition allows members to achieve better results than working alone, but inevitably requires greater commitment and effort. Every coalition is different, but the East African experience reveals key lessons applicable to all:

1. *Build relationships proactively within the coalition.* For the sustainability of the coalition, it is important to address members' concerns continuously and to create a purpose that each member can support or identify with. Members' individual goals need space in the coalition agenda if they are to feel useful. Ignoring concerns can lead to a revolt within the coalition. However, giving any member more space or attention than others can upset the coalition. The convener requires strong leadership skills to balance this need and direct the membership constantly toward the coalition's common mission. This is the "give and take" concept of any relationship.

2. *Ensure members' institutional commitment at the highest level.* FoTAPP's membership is institution based. This has posed a challenge in the implementation of decisions, as every decision must be further discussed at individual institution level before approval, resulting in significant delays and sometimes stagnation where a quorum cannot be achieved. FoTAPP also suffered setbacks when a member's representative left that institution, taking with them the institutional memory. This requires an effective induction for the new representative, and the time required for them to understand how the coalition works sometimes causes projects to stall.

   There is a need for balance, in which institutions commit to the coalition and have more than one employee engaged in its work. This strategy, which enhances participation in the coalition's activities, is achieved through winning buy-in from the member's top management. This then cushions the coalition so that when an individual representative leaves a member organization, the transition is made smoother through replacing the outgoing representative with another employee of the member institution who was already aware of the coalition's work. Having institutions as members, as opposed to a coalition of individuals, also has the benefit of bringing credibility to a coalition and attracting recognition by other stakeholders.

3. *Have a clear coalition agenda.* Where the participation of an organization is checkered, its representatives may not understand the mandate and the scope of the work. This can result in attempts to introduce individual organization's mandates into the coalition mandate or delays in arriving at consensus on an issue.

Accelerating Health Reforms through Collective Action • http://dx.doi.org/10.1596/978-1-4648-0287-4

4. *Ensure sustainable financial resources.* The coalition has to continuously remind itself of the need to be sustainable, with or without external financial support. One way is to engage with beneficiaries (such as the relevant departments within the Ministry of Health, citizen groups, etc.) on the impact of the coalition's work. This has strong potential to achieve their buy-in.

5. *Emphasize the common goal.* It is important to remain aware that the multistakeholder approach may be difficult for partners outside the coalition to understand. Questions may include how the coalition can work with a member partner whom it is meant to monitor. This issue was addressed through continuous emphasis of the beneficiaries of the coalition—Kenya's citizens—and ensuring that all work undertaken was geared toward improving the population's health rather than "correcting" any member organization's faults. Keep reminding members about the greater goal that all are working to achieve: access to medicines at affordable prices for the country's citizens.

Notes

1. In Kenya, under the National Health Sector Strategic Plan II (2005–2012) the government (Ministry of Health) has established virtual "drawing rights" for health facilities to move toward the "pull" system of supply, in which facilities order their required supplies and commodities based on actual need rather than receiving centrally determined numbers of medicine kits (referred to as the "push" system of supply). See Ramana, Gandham N. V., Rose Chepkoech, and Netsanet Walelign Workie. 2013. *Improving Universal Primary Health Care by Kenya: A Case Study of the Health Sector Services Fund* (UNICO Studies Series 5). Washington DC: The World Bank. http://www-wds.worldbank.org/external/default/WDSContentServer/WDSP/IB/2013/02/04/000425962_20130204110301/Rendered/PDF/750020NWP0Box30ry0Health0Care0KENYA.pdf (accessed June 3, 2014).

2. Calculated at the average pay for short-term consultants, $250 per day.

3. Staff related costs such as salary, revenue generated, transport costs.

4. The National Taxpayers Association (NTA) is an independent, nonpartisan organization focused on promoting good governance in Kenya through citizen empowerment, enhancing public service delivery, and partnership building. One of its key objectives, linked to FoTAPP's goals, is to ensure that taxpayers' money is used to deliver quality public services for all Kenyans.

5. The Mobile-phone Drug Tracking System (MDTS) was piloted as part of KEMSA's e-mobile system. This system allows KEMSA to inform customers and health care stakeholders more accurately and efficiently about the amount of essential medicines and medical supplies being consumed nationwide, and the stock levels, in order to serve all Kenyans equally. The use of mobile technology allows each facility to send orders to KEMSA and report on consumption data, thereby facilitating proper planning and forecasting of commodities.

CHAPTER 4

Branching Out and Bearing Fruits

Deciding and Implementing Coalition Activities:
Collaborative Action in Uganda

Emmanuel Higenyi, Jacqueline Idusso, and Robinah Kaitiritimba

Introduction

The test of any coalition is its ability to work on concrete initiatives directly linked to the attainment of its objectives. In the context of health reforms, successful coalitions are those able to leverage their members' respective competitive advantages to design interventions that catalzye change.

This chapter describes Medicines Transparency Alliance (MeTA) Uganda's experience in working collaboratively to generate the evidence necessary to inform policy making. It outlines the key steps taken, including approaches for setting priorities, developing civil society capacity, and implementing country action plans and joint initiatives. From these activities valuable lessons emerged in sustaining collaborative action, most notably:

- The importance of maintaining coalition cohesion
- The centrality of the coalition's credibility and legitimacy in creating the space for it to contribute to reforms
- The need for high-level political buy-in
- The opportunities that obstacles can present for innovation and creativity
- The need to recognize and respect stakeholder sensitivities in order to establish an enabling environment for cooperation.

MeTA Uganda has accomplished much as a coalition since its inception in 2009. However, this chapter gives more prominence to the World Bank Institute (WBI)-facilitated interventions, as this publication is primarily intended to share experiences based on WBI's support for coalition building at country and regional levels.

The Ugandan Context

Uganda is classified as a Least Developed Country by the United Nations and a low-income country by the World Bank (United Nation 2004). The country's economy is predominantly agricultural, although the service sector constitutes a significant portion of gross domestic product (GDP) (Mangeni 2012). Approximately 80 percent of the population lives in rural areas with limited access to health care services, potable water, and sanitation facilities. The United Nations Children's Fund (UNICEF) estimates that 38 percent of the population (that is, over 12 million people) survives on less than US$1.25 a day.

Health Sector Structure and Key Actors

The Ugandan health system is generally public-sector driven, with a very strong private nonprofit component whose service delivery model mirrors that of the public sector. Services and commodities in public health facilities are generally free, while private nonprofit health facilities provide services and commodities on a cost recovery basis.

The provision of health services is decentralized, with districts and health subdistricts playing a key role in the delivery and management of health services at local levels. Health facilities are structured into national and regional referral hospitals, general hospitals, health centers (levels II–IV), and village health teams (health center level I).

There are three levels of supervision: (i) central level institutions such as the Ministry of Health (MoH); (ii) local governments, such as District Health Offices; and (iii) hospitals and lower level health units. While systems for supervision, monitoring, and evaluation exist, there are enormous challenges associated with monitoring and supervision. For instance, Area Team visits (officer appointed by the Ministry of Health and based at regional hospitals) have been irregular due to the late release of funds, insufficient funds, and inadequate transport arrangements. They have also been ineffective due to insufficient feedback to the districts (Uganda Health Sector Strategic Plan III 2010/11–2014/15).

The key actors within the health sector are as follows:

The Ministry of Health: The managerial and service delivery activities within the health sector are based on the mission, vision, policies, and strategic plans articulated by MoH. The ministry takes the lead in policy formulation, resource mobilization, program implementation, and monitoring overall performance of the sector. In delivery of its mandate, it recognizes the contribution made by civil society organizations (CSOs) and the private sector, which participate in the formulation of health policies and strategic plans under the Public-Private Partnership for Health (PPPH).

Civil Society Organizations: CSOs perform a monitoring role in the budgeting process and implementation of government commitments. In so doing, they promote downward accountability, and mobilize and sensitize health consumers and politicians regarding key health matters. Some achievements in the sector have been attained through civil society involvement, such as increased funding for maternal and child medicines, as well as recruitment of more health workers. These successes highlight the importance of collaboration.

Health Unit Management Committee: For management and governance, each health facility has a Health Unit Management Committee (HUMC) or Hospital Board, in addition to the head of the facility. Committee or board members are elected by the community, while the committee or board secretary is the facility head. The HUMC or board acts as the voice of the community within the health facility, and is responsible for holding health facility management teams accountable for the efficient use of medicines and other resources. Among its duties is the verification of medicines arriving at a facility. These governance structures also act as redress mechanisms for community members on issues related to service quality and the availability of medicines.

Private Sector: The private sector also works in partnership with the public sector to deliver services such as medicine distribution and immunization. The PPPH, approved by the cabinet in 2011, facilitates the coexistence of both public and private sectors in a manner that is integrated and coordinated.

Development Partners: Development partners play a key role by providing policy and implementation support. Through initiatives like the Sector Wide Approach (SWAP), they coordinate efforts to better leverage respective comparative advantages in order to improve health outcomes.

Health Sector Hurdles and Opportunities

Uganda's health system faces a variety of challenges. Three core issues reflected in the current Health Sector Strategic Investment Plan (HSSIP) are as follows: (i) access to essential medicines; (ii) human resource constraints, and (iii) health care financing.

Access to Medicines: Access to essential medicines is an important priority for the Ugandan government. The National Health Plan seeks to "ensure that essential, efficacious, safe, quality and affordable medicines are available and used rationally at all times in Uganda". Achieving this goal requires, among other things, the suitable pricing of essential medicines at public facilities to ensure that the poor can obtain lifesaving medicines; strengthening of the supply chain to ensure that medicines are readily available to meet patients' needs; the development and maintenance of infrastructure to transport and store medicines in line with international best practice; and the training of a workforce to manage the pharmaceutical supply chain.

Despite recent reforms to enhance access to essential medicines, the health sector still faces significant challenges, including high stock-out rates in public health facilities—with an average duration of 72.6 days compared with 7.6 days in mission facilities (HSSIP). The HSSIP indicates that only 30 percent of the

Essential Medicines and Health Supplies list required for the basic health package is provided for in the national budget; global initiatives provide the bulk of resources needed for malaria, human immunodeficiency virus (HIV) and acquired immune deficiency syndrome (AIDS), tuberculosis, vaccines, and reproductive health. Delays in procurement, poor record-keeping, and poor quantification and late orders by facilities contribute to a waste of medicines in the public sector. The cost of medicines also remains too high for many citizens—particularly the poor. Medicines in private facilities are estimated to be 3–5 times more expensive than in public facilities.

Human resource constraints: Like many developing economies, Uganda lacks an adequate, skilled health care workforce to support a growing disease burden. The 2012–13 Report of the Parliamentary Committee on Health indicates a doctor-to-patient ratio of 1:24,725 and nurse/midwife-to-patient ratio of 1:11,000. On average, Uganda has a health worker to patient ratio of 1:818 compared with the World Health Organization (WHO) benchmark of 1:439 (Namaganda, McMahan, and Oketcho 2012). The report also shows that only 58 percent of health care positions are filled: Absenteeism and the inability to retain health workers—particularly at the lower levels of care—are contributing factors.

Health Financing: Out-of-pocket health care financing represents 54 percent of total health expenditure in Uganda (MeTA 2010; Parliament of Uganda 2013). The government makes a contribution toward the delivery of health care services; however, the budget allocation for the health sector is significantly below the threshold of 15 percent stated in the Abuja Declaration. In the 2013–14 fiscal year, for instance, Uganda allocated 8.7 percent of the national budget to health (directly through the MoH).

The proportion of the population covered by some form of health insurance is also very small, at 3 percent (United Nations 2004), meaning that payment for health care is made at the point of need. Given the large proportion of Ugandans living below the poverty line, high health care costs directly impact their ability to access quality health services, including medicines.

To address health sector challenges and accelerate the country's efforts to achieve the targets of the Millennium Development Goals, several reforms have been put in place. These include efforts to achieve quality, equity, efficiency, and effectiveness by (i) bringing health services closer to citizens with the creation of more health centers; (ii) devolving health services to local government authorities in order to increase community participation, promote social accountability, and enhance responsiveness to local needs; (iii) promulgating new policies including the National Health Policy and the HSSIP; and (iv) subsidizing the cost of primary health care services with initiatives such as the abolition of user fees.

In line with the broad reform agenda, the HSSIP II (which covers 2010–15) is aggressively targeting (i) scaling up critical interventions already underway (such as initiatives linked to maternal and child health); (ii) improving access to and demand for health services (including essential medicines); (iii) accelerating quality and safety improvements; (iv) improving efficiency and budget effectiveness; and (v) deepening health stewardship through strategic partnerships and collaborative initiatives.

The Pharmaceutical Subsector

Uganda has an established policy and regulatory framework for pharmaceuticals, implemented by the National Drug Authority (NDA). The authority is responsible for regulating the pharmaceutical market, licensing premises, issuing drug information, pharmacovigilance, quality assurance, import permissions, and disposal of expired medicines. However, it has a limited capacity with insufficient outreach (HSSIP II).

The National Medical Store (NMS) is a parastatal organization responsible for procuring and storing medicines and distributing them to public health facilities. The Joint Medical Store (JMS) procures and distributes to faith-based and other nonprofit health facilities. A number of private distributors and wholesalers supply medicines to private service providers. Other stakeholders include the parliamentary committee on health; the Ministries of Health and of Finance, Planning and Economic Development; local districts; health facilities; civil society; and development partners.

According to HSSIP II, approximately 940 billion Ugandan shillings (UGX) is required to cover the national need for pharmaceuticals, health supplies, and commodities annually. Of this amount, 65.5 percent would be spent at community and district level—primarily on HIV and AIDS, as well as malaria medication and commodities. Essential medicines and health supplies take up 12.5 percent of total costs.

The pharmaceutical subsector has also undergone several reforms in recent years. These include the centralization of medicine procurement and distribution through the NMS; increased funding for essential medicines and health supplies; the embossment of medicines to ensure authenticity; and establishment of the Medicines and Health Services Monitoring Unit. The sector has also adopted an "informed push" system for medical supplies, based on standard kits developed by district health officers in consultation with health facility heads, and issued from the center to lower-level health facilities. A "last mile" delivery system[1] has been introduced for consignments, which is intended to reduce delays and optimize the use of transportation resources.

Several challenges remain, however, including issues such as the absence of price control regimes for the private sector, inadequate legal controls or incentives, and no standard operating procedure for public procurement agencies vis-à-vis their interactions with suppliers (MeTA 2010). In addition, inadequate infrastructure for quality control testing of medicines at ports of entry also compromises the effectiveness of the drug regulatory authority, leading to delays in the release of medicines and medical supplies to market, which affects availability and accessibility. Public facilities, especially at the district level, lack the capacity to collect, analyze, interpret, and use logistical and other health information effectively for pharmaceutical procurement and supply chain management (PSM) processes (MoH 2012). All these challenges are exacerbated by inadequate sharing and analysis of logistical, demographic, and epidemiologic information among the various actors in the pharmaceutical sector.

The inability to share information and work effectively through a unified approach makes it increasingly difficult to develop sustainable solutions to persistent challenges and to hold service providers accountable.

An Opportunity for Collaboration: The Existing Multistakeholder Landscape

As part of its reform agenda, the Government of Uganda has prioritized the need to engage several stakeholders in the process of formulating health policies and monitoring their implementation. It recognizes that addressing the system failures inherent in the sector will require the mobilization of various resources (technical and human), and the exploration of new approaches to solving perennial issues. The HSSIP underscores the need for the MoH to strengthen interagency collaboration, as well as engage the private sector and civil society in resolving sectoral challenges. Existing examples of government-led multistakeholder initiatives include the PPPH, the Health Policy Advisory Committee, Technical Working Groups, and Regional Stakeholders Fora. These groups debate a variety of issues, ranging from agreeing the strategic priorities of the sector to coordination of health service delivery at district level.

Within the area of pharmaceutical procurement in particular, the MoH has a track record of partnering with CSOs and development partners such as the World Health Organization (WHO), the Danish International Development Agency (DANIDA), and Health Action International (HAI). Joint activities include designing health policies, monitoring access to essential medicines, and leading advocacy efforts. While these interventions have enhanced collaborative engagement, they have tended to be ad hoc, focused on specific issues and activities. This meant that there was clear opportunity for the creation of a multistakeholder process that would be both sustainable and that would be *actively* involved in the entire value chain of reform processes—from design and implementation to monitoring and evaluation.

The Medicines Transparency Alliance (MeTA)

MeTA is an international multistakeholder initiative which operates in seven countries, including Uganda, and whose aim is to "improve access, availability and affordability of medicines for the one-third of the world's population to whom access is currently denied." Centered on information sharing and collective action, the initiative is premised on a theory of change which holds that open publication, discussion, and analysis of information about the medicine supply chain by three major stakeholder groups—the government, the private sector, and civil society—will lead to a better understanding of problems, create greater incentives to pioneer change, and promote greater responsibility and account-ability among those needed to instigate these changes ("Medicines Transparency Alliance: A Review of the Pilot"). The anticipated result is increased access to medicines for the most vulnerable sectors of society. This theory of change is illustrated in figure 4.1.

MeTA Uganda

MeTA Uganda ("the coalition") was launched in 2009, becoming one of the first multistakeholder initiatives to focus solely on improving access to medi-cines at the country level (MeTA Uganda Workplan [2012–15]). Prior to the coalition's creation, the MoH had collaborated with agencies such as DANIDA to enhance the rational use of medicines, and participated in a tripartite group to monitor access to medicines, along with WHO and HAI Africa (represented at the country level by the Coalition for Health Promotion and Social Development [HEPS], a health rights organization that advocates for increased access to affordable essential medicines for poor and vulnerable people in Uganda).

The initiative was the first to bring together a multiplicity of actors and stake-holders including the MoH, medicines agencies, wholesalers, manufacturers, faith-based organizations, CSOs, and academia (MeTA Uganda Phase 2). The MeTA Uganda initiative was innovative in its narrow focus on access to medi-cines, and emphasis on generating evidence, facilitating the disclosure of informa-tion and building the capacity of CSOs to lead advocacy efforts. It also had much broader stakeholder participation than existing groups, which were primarily coordinated through the MoH and tended to be dominated by the public sector. Given MeTA's independence, the stakeholder group could take a more critical perspective on reform issues and could also exercise greater flexibility in its choice of priorities and activities. The coordination provided by both WHO and HAI Africa allowed knowledge exchange and peer-to-peer learning with other countries undergoing similar health sector reforms. It also elevated the coalition's activities to a global level, providing important visibility and recognition for efforts implemented at country level.

Figure 4.1 The Medicines Transparency Alliance Model

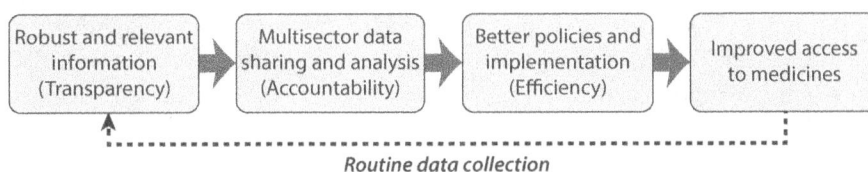

Robust and relevant information (Transparency) → Multisector data sharing and analysis (Accountability) → Better policies and implementation (Efficiency) → Improved access to medicines

Routine data collection

Source: MeTA 2010.

MeTA Uganda's goal is to increase access to essential medicines, especially for the poor and vulnerable. The initiative has a 12-member governing council, a three-member secretariat (representing the public sector, the private sector, and civil society), and a coordinator. The council is the governing body and is responsible for overseeing all the management and financial activities of participating stakeholders, as well as MeTA Uganda's national secretariat. The secretariat consists of the MoH, the Uganda Pharmaceutical Manufacturers Association, and HEPS. The chair of the MeTA council is rotated between these three representative groups, and the coordinator of MeTA Uganda appointed by the council on contract to assist the national secretariat.

MeTA also includes representation from the NDA, NMS, Makerere University (a public university in Kampala training graduate pharmacists), the Pharmaceutical Society of Uganda (an umbrella body for pharmacists), HEPS-Uganda, the Private Pharmaceutical Manufacturers Association, the Uganda National Health Consumers Organization (UNHCO), JMS, and Medical Access Uganda Limited. The WHO, the World Bank Group, and DANIDA are also members of the multistakeholder group.

Working Together: Setting Priorities for Initial Steps

Setting Priorities—MeTA Phase I

While MeTA's broad objective was defined at the global level, each country had to design a work plan independently and set priorities in line with its own reform agenda. For Uganda, Phase I of MeTA's activity (2008–10) meant demonstrating the capacity of multiple stakeholders to work together effectively; providing input on legislative reforms; advocating the disclosure of information, and building CSO capacity to understand technical issues, as well as to acquire skillsets in communication and third-party monitoring (MeTA Phase 01 Pilot).

These priorities were agreed for three main reasons: (i) they represented "low-hanging fruit" where the initiative could achieve some early wins and successes; (ii) the development of critical health sector policies at the time (notably the National Health Policy II, HSSIP II, and the National Pharmaceutical Sector Strategic Plan II) provided an excellent opportunity for MeTA Uganda to provide input on policy reforms; and (iii) the initiative recognized that civil society lacked the capacity to engage effectively on technical pharmaceutical issues and would therefore have to be trained in order to participate more constructively in policy dialogue, advocate information disclosure, and monitor sector performance.

With high-level support from the MoH, which was a primary stakeholder in the coalition, MeTA Uganda was able to achieve important successes during Phase I, which would help set the agenda for Phase II. Key achievements included the following:

1. *Provision of a platform for broadened multistakeholder engagement and inclusive decision making*: MeTA Uganda facilitated the inclusion of different stakeholder

groups in the MoH planning process. For the first time, the ministry invited the private sector and CSOs to participate in the weeklong review of the first National Pharmaceutical Sector Strategic Plan (NPSSP I), the outcome of which informed the development of the five-year NPSSP II (2009–10 to 2013–14).

2. *Disclosure of information:* MeTA Uganda supported the NDA in making the database of registered medicines available on its website. It advocated enhancements such as a search feature, which has allowed citizens to query the database for information on the registration status of a medicine, pharmacy, retailer, or manufacturer.

3. *Increased advocacy:* The prominence given through MeTA to issues affecting the availability of medicines, and the coordinating role the initiative has played, have help galvanize CSOs to advocate for improved access to essential medicines. With capacity building and the strategic partnerships offered through MeTA, CSOs have been able to gain entry into relatively insular public institutions, as well as gain the technical expertise to lead efforts such as the "Stop Stock-Outs" campaign.

These achievements were very important for MeTA Uganda, helping to demonstrate an increasing willingness to work through collaborative mechanisms. They also strengthened relationships with key stakeholders (in the public sector, the private sector, and civil society), as well as helping to build credibility and legitimacy for the new coalition. However, it became evident that for MeTA Uganda to have a more sustained impact on the policy agenda, it would be important for it to undertake projects that could generate evidence for informed decision making and policy reform. This would require additional time, financial and technical resources, the commitment of all stakeholders, and agreement on the kinds of data to collect.

Setting Priorities Phase II

In 2010, as MeTA Uganda was completing Phase I of implementation, the World Bank Institute (WBI) approached its membership to discuss a proposed new initiative, *Improving Governance in Pharmaceutical Procurement and Supply Chain Management.* The proposed initiative aimed to "improve access to essential medicines by promoting transparency and accountability in pharmaceutical procurement and supply chain management". WBI sought MeTA Uganda's input on the proposed initiative as part of a comprehensive country-level stakeholder mapping exercise.

There were clear synergies between MeTA Uganda's priorities and the focus of the new WBI-led initiative. However, although focused purely on PSM issues, the initiative was more action oriented and leveraged World Bank Group capabilities in technical assistance on broad governance issues, including social accountability and third-party monitoring.

Accelerating Health Reforms through Collective Action • http://dx.doi.org/10.1596/978-1-4648-0287-4

MeTA Uganda saw clear value in collaborating with WBI. This would allow it broader scope to tackle PSM issues, viewed as central to addressing the challenges in access to medicines. WBI could provide capacity development to help MeTA Uganda better address the political economy of reform and design the robust communications strategy necessary to promote change and mobilize resources. It could also help MeTA Uganda design and implement results-oriented action plans to advance its overall objectives. The collaboration would prevent the duplication of efforts, while building on successes achieved so far.

In April 2011, a few months after the consultations with WBI, MeTA Uganda participated in a World Bank-led regional workshop in Nairobi, Kenya. Its objectives included helping multistakeholder coalitions established in Kenya, Tanzania, and Uganda develop country action plans that would guide their activities over the short and medium term. Facilitated discussions on challenges in the pharmaceutical supply sector helped to reinforce the value of multistakeholder processes and to percolate ideas on how to overcome barriers to change effectively. The workshop included thought-provoking presentations organized within the Flagship Framework,[2] an integrated approach to help countries think and debate in new ways about how to improve performance and efficiency in health systems. Given its utility and broad usage, the framework was adapted within the context of pharmaceutical PSM. Importantly, the workshop exposed participants to innovative Information and Communications Technology (ICT)-enabled interventions designed to help stakeholders to better track medicine availability. These innovations struck MeTA Uganda as offering a clear opportunity to accelerate PSM reforms.

In addition, the workshop provided critical tools and resources, such as the Rapid Results Approach[3] framework, to guide coalitions in identifying priority areas of joint intervention and to develop action-oriented plans for attaining short-term targets. It also facilitated the development of a regional community of practice that could share insights, experiences, and lessons on implementation challenges, as well as codevelop ideas on new approaches for accelerating PSM reforms.[4]

Key MeTA Uganda stakeholders participated in the Nairobi workshop, including MoH, NMS, NDA, JMS, the Public Procurement and Disposal Agency, civil society groups, and the media. For this core group, the workshop provided a valuable opportunity to expand the scope of MeTA's work program. The group developed a prototype action plan focusing on three main elements: (i) an ICT-enabled tracking system for monitoring medicine availability at the health facility level; (ii) improving information flow about PSM issues; and (iii) empowering citizens through targeted capacity development on social accountability.

These priorities were a logical follow-up to Phase I, an assessment of which had shown the need for more focused interventions that could generate an evidence base for policy dialogue. ICT-enabled monitoring would generate data, while increased advocacy around information flow, as well as citizen engagement, could place pressure on service providers to be transparent and accountable.

Capacity Development

Capacity development was delivered through a combined effort by MeTA Global, MeTA Uganda, and the WBI. MeTA Uganda recognized civil society capacity development as integral to facilitating the design and implementation of joint activities. Civil society groups tended to lack the technical PSM knowledge necessary to contribute effectively to the coalition, balance asymmetries of information, achieve more equality between coalition members, and facilitate constructive engagement with technical agencies such as MoH or medicines institutions. MeTA Uganda envisioned a role around social accountability and third-party monitoring, and therefore viewed it as necessary to train and equip CSOs appropriately. Technical training would also be needed in order to enhance the legitimacy and credibility of CSOs, many of which would be leading advocacy efforts around access to medicines.

MeTA Uganda therefore trained civil society groups in multistakeholder processes, transparency, accountability, research approaches, advocacy campaigns, communications, and negotiation. Given the nature of government-CSO relations, which in some contexts could be tense, it was important to guide nonstate actors in approaches that would encourage rather than prevent partnership with the public sector. Media engagement strategies helped CSO groups to lead advocacy efforts around the rational use of medicines, while training in communication guided the development of briefs on ongoing policy debates.

These capacity development efforts were complemented by workshops on the roles and responsibilities of different agencies in the pharmaceutical sector. Designed in partnership with medicines institutions such as NMS, these workshops covered topics including access to medicines, and their pricing, availability, and promotion. MeTA Uganda played an important facilitator role, both by inviting additional CSOs into the coalition and by introducing them to the key medicines institutions.

The MeTA global secretariat also facilitated peer-to-peer learning and coaching between the various MeTA pilot countries in order to enhance knowledge exchange on approaches that were proving successful for CSO capacity development. Field visits to agencies such as the NDA, JMS, local health care facilities, and private facilities complemented the training, providing invaluable learning about internal processes, as well as health care delivery platforms.

At the regional level, a select number of civil society groups also participated in a Training of Trainers (ToT) workshop in Tanzania, convened by WBI and focused on using social accountability mechanisms to enhance PSM governance. Civil society groups which had participated subsequently trained additional groups at country level, with guidance from a ToT manual. To sustain capacity development as a core feature of the regional coalition-building initiative, WBI continued to organize annual regional workshops focused on tackling implementation challenges facing the coalitions. These addressed issues such as effective stakeholder mapping, strategic communications, and the political economy of reform. This frequent and consistent training helped MeTA Uganda and the coalitions in Kenya and Tanzania to stay on course, as well as enabling them to quickly address any emerging challenges.

In May 2011, MeTA Uganda hosted a policy dialogue with representatives of medicines institutions, notably NMS, MoH, and JMS. The event served as an important forum for candid conversation between government and civil society groups on the opportunities and challenges associated with PSM. It also introduced monitoring tools already tested in the health sector (such as community score cards, public partnership expenditure monitoring tools, citizen report cards, social audits, and budget analysis). The dialogue, the first of its kind, was especially well received by NMS, which requested follow-up consultations in order to keep the conversation open and promote the free flow of information. During the discussion, the NMS General Manager noted, "It's a shame that I am meeting some of the most active health sector CSOs for the first time. We should have a regular meeting at NMS from now on—that is my offer." These comments reinforced the NMS commitment to working through the MeTA framework to address PSM reforms, and also provided the space for broader engagement with CSO groups.

These activities have been critical for strengthening civil society capacity within MeTA Uganda. However, it must also be acknowledged that capacity development efforts have—by their nature—been ongoing and issue driven, and have involved a variety of other interventions such as peer-to-peer learning.

Putting Plans into Action

The priority areas for intervention identified at the Nairobi workshop (ICT-based tracking of medicines, citizen empowerment, and information disclosure) were in alignment with broader MeTA objectives and HSSIP. However, it was important to follow the workshop with specific country-level interventions. Firstly, it was essential to secure broader buy-in from all key stakeholders for implementation of these priorities. This would involve a series of consultations to generate country ownership of the plan. It was then essential to reach out to high-level policy makers—such as the permanent secretary—to gain the necessary political support for the planned activities. Finally, it was critical to mobilize resources for a new set of activities which had not been budgeted for previously.

Over the course of several months, MeTA Uganda was able to make important advancements in implementing its stated priorities. To increase citizen empowerment, it participated in the ToT workshop on PSM and Social Accountability (referenced above). Using the ToT manual, the coalition trained CSOs at country level, strengthening their capacity to understand fundamental technical PSM issues and the need to monitor the supply chain, as well as learning about the tools and resources available for community-led and citizen reporting. Efforts around information disclosure had already been initiated through MeTA Uganda Phase I. Having gained traction in pushing reforms in this domain, the coalition sought to continue its work, albeit with a broader cross-section of stakeholders such as NMS.

However, it proved challenging to implement the first priority identified in Nairobi: the design and use of a standardized, innovative ICT platform for tracking medicines, which could also be institutionalized in the MoH. A primary step to achieving this priority was to understand the ICT landscape in the health sector. This meant determining how many initiatives were *eHealth*[5] and *mHealth*[6] focused and how MeTA Uganda could leverage what existed to help achieve its own objectives. The coalition conducted a scan of the sector, which coincided with the Ministry's own investigation of eHealth and mHealth initiatives.

It quickly became apparent that the fragmented and large number of existing ICT-related initiatives in the sector first needed to be reviewed and harmonized. This step would be necessary before MeTA could begin to design and develop an ICT platform for tracking medicines. In the interim, in January 2012, the MoH placed a moratorium on all new eHealth and mHealth initiatives, to allow time to develop a National eHealth Policy to better harmonize ICT-enabled efforts, as well as provide some coherence to their development and sustainability. While the rationale for this decision was sound, it would ultimately impact MeTA Uganda's ability to move quickly in implementing the key priority in its action plan. As a result, the coalition, after careful consideration, dropped ICT as one of its focus areas.

In April 2012, WBI convened a regional workshop in Kampala to respond to implementation challenges facing all three coalitions. MeTA Uganda now had to identify an alternative to ICT-enabled interventions, which until that point had been central to its action plan. The workshop had four main objectives: to (i) share implementation experiences, challenges, and lessons learned; (ii) explore potential solutions to implementation barriers; (iii) reprioritize areas for action in each country; and (iv) build skills in adaptive leadership, strategic communication, and negotiations.

For MeTA Uganda, the workshop had two main advantages. It reinvigorated members of the coalition, providing new perspectives on dealing with challenges in the political economy, and equipping stakeholders to secure buy-in from actors whose support would be critical for program success. It also allowed a re-examination of coalition priorities, emphasizing the need to generate evidence for informed policy debate.

During the workshop, MeTA Uganda reinforced its commitment to empowering citizens and promoting information disclosure. The coalition agreed, however, that while it was important to leverage ICT-enabled technology to generate evidence, in the short term, more traditional mechanisms would be expeditious, more politically palatable and cost effective.

Generating Evidence to Inform Policy

Identifying the Gaps

The process towards generating evidence to inform policymaking was multifaceted and systematic. It was an advantage that all three coalitions in Kenya,

Tanzania, and Uganda had prioritized data collection as a core activity. This allowed WBI to leverage both technical and financial resources to support the coalitions in designing and testing relevant tools.

The first phase of the data collection process involved a thorough and extensive desk review of monitoring tools available in the public domain and which would be relevant for the kinds of PSM monitoring activities that the coalitions envisioned. Recognizing that data collection had to be responsive to the needs of the sector, each coalition worked with stakeholders to customize the tools. For this reason, while the coalitions used similar tools, ultimately the data collected served different purposes in line with health sector priorities in each country. MeTA Uganda had three main areas of focus in data collection:

- *Client Satisfaction with Health Services*: The prioritization of data collection coincided with the MoH review of its monitoring and evaluation plan as part of the broader strategic planning process for 2010/11–2014/15. The review process revealed a gap in data on client satisfaction with health service delivery. While the ministry had extensive data collected from sources such as the Demographic and Health Surveys, it specifically sought data from citizens— viewed as an important outcome indicator for gauging the efficacy of ongoing reforms.

  While health service delivery was not MeTA Uganda's primary focus area, the coalition recognized that it was important to be both opportunistic and responsive to the needs of the Ministry. By broadening the scope of the data collection exercise to cover client satisfaction with health services, the coalition could both build social capital within the MoH, as well as gain buy-in for other efforts linked specifically to access to medicines.

- *Pharmaceutical Supply Chain Management:* Given MeTA Uganda's mission, data collection would naturally have to examine pharmaceutical supply chain management issues, as well as medicine availability at the facility level. As the NMS had recently implemented reforms, including improvements to medicine delivery schedules, it was important to follow up these efforts to determine their efficacy, as well as to elicit feedback from both demand- and supply-side clients. With NMS, JMS, and the Public Procurement Disposal of Public Assets Authority (PPDPA) as key stakeholders, this was also an area where data collected would have a clear use and could directly inform enhancements to bureaucratic and administrative processes.

- *Citizen Empowerment:* MeTA Uganda had a track record in community-level engagement. Two strong CSOs—the Uganda National Health Consumers/ Users Organization and the Coalition for Health Promotion and Social Development—had initiated several studies in the past on access to medicines and client satisfaction. Given their extensive experience at community level, the coalition believed that any type of joint activity would also need to focus on assessing citizen empowerment and designing interventions that could empower clients to advocate for better health service delivery and to hold providers accountable.

In Tanzania, the Multistakeholder Group on Pharmaceutical Procurement (MSG-Pharma) prioritized data collection around compliance with public procurement processes. This decision was based on the strong relationships with the Public Procurement Regulatory Authority, which was a key stakeholder in the coalition and had a particular interest in assessing how districts were procuring medicines. Given high levels of stock-out rates, the coalition also sought to monitor stock levels at district hospitals, hoping to triangulate data from the hospital level with that from the district procurement offices to determine whether there were any linkages between procurement processes and outcomes in medicine availability.

In Kenya, the focus of the FoTAPP coalition was on citizen monitoring of health services, as well as FoTAPP monitoring stock levels of essential medicines. There was also a unique opportunity to join forces with the Health Sector Services Project, managed through the Ministry of Health. This project had implemented a variety of social accountability measures in selected pilot sites. It was useful to the coalition's data collection efforts to follow up with these sites to determine the efficacy of the interventions. As a result, Kenya's data collection focused strongly on examining citizen knowledge of rights related to health services, comparing data from sites where the project had implemented interventions with data from control sites.

In designing tools for data generation, all three coalitions leveraged opportunities not only to work together as partners but also to learn from their respective experiences. A conscious division of labor ensured that each coalition developed a set of tools for which it had technical competency. Tanzania developed the supply-side tools, such as the procurement monitoring tool and stock monitoring tools. In Kenya, FoTAPP developed the citizen monitoring tool, while MeTA Uganda created the citizen empowerment tool. The data collection activities were also staggered, to allow coalitions to learn from the experiences and insights of their peers. This ongoing learning helped coalitions avoid some of the common pitfalls such as logistical challenges, while use of the online community of practice, http://www.enepp.net, helped facilitate the shared development and tailoring of ideas.

Designing the Tools

In October 2013, representatives of all three coalitions convened in Tanzania for a Technical Working Group meeting hosted by WBI. The meeting aimed to (i) develop an appropriate monitoring and evaluation (M&E) framework to guide the data collection process; (ii) review, revise, and finalize a consolidated tool; and (iii) devise a strategy for the rollout of the tools, agreeing on sample size, pilot sites, duration of data collection and analysis. The meeting generated a completed M&E framework, along with a finalized Client Satisfaction Survey and Procurement Monitoring Tool, and a draft Stock Monitoring Tool.

At country level, MeTA Uganda finalized these tools in consultation with other coalition members—notably MoH, NMS, and JMS. Through the leadership of UNHCO, the coalition also piloted the tools and trained personnel to administer them during a full launch. In recognition of the local priorities, MeTA Uganda developed a citizen empowerment tool which sought to determine the extent to which users of health services provided feedback (in particular, filed complaints) on poor health care delivery, and their knowledge and usage of existing redress mechanisms and accountability structures. It also created a key informant questionnaire to interview several stakeholders within the Ministry of Finance, NMS, JMS, and development partners, to gather information on the challenges associated with PSM and potential opportunities for implementing sustainable solutions.

The test pilot proved successful, gaining endorsement from the MoH and the medicines institutions, and approval from the MeTA council for the coalition to proceed with putting together a team that could manage the design and delivery of the data collection exercise. Key stakeholders from both government and civil society committed to providing technical resources in the form of skilled personnel to administer the surveys. This way, the coalition leveraged the knowledge and expertise of its own membership, drawing on JMS and ministry staff to develop a draft methodology for the survey.

However, MeTA Uganda was concerned about two main issues regarding the data collection exercise: (i) how to make the results acceptable to key stakeholders such as NMS, MoH, service providers, and local government authorities; and (ii) how to incentivize relevant stakeholders to implement recommendations emerging from the exercise. In response, it was agreed to include all stakeholder groups in every stage of the data collection process—from design and administration to validation and dissemination of findings. This intense level of collaboration was necessary to ensure the credibility of the exercise, acceptance for the study rationale and results, and stakeholders' commitment to implementing remedial actions.

Harness Skills for an Effective Team

A distinctive feature of the data collection exercise in Uganda is that it was truly participatory. While the ministry and medicines agencies had historically collected data and performed diagnostics on a number of medicine-related issues, this was the first time that all the agencies along with CSOs had designed and administered a survey of such breadth and depth. From training data collectors to administering the survey, validating the findings, and sharing the results publicly, all the key stakeholders were actively involved.

The design team consisted of NMS, JMS, MoH, HEPS, UNHCO, and the Africa Freedom of Information Center (AFIC). The criteria for joining the design team were technical expertise in PSM; research experience and the ability to collect data from the field effectively; the availability of skilled personnel to participate in training and supervise data collection over a two-week period; and legitimacy and credibility within the socio-political sphere.

Each member of the core team held a comparative advantage: both NMS and JMS brought technical expertise in PSM issues and could provide guidance on the design and administration of the stock monitoring tools and key informant interview. The NMS general manager facilitated the training of data collectors, explaining pharmaceutical supply chain functions, the roles and responsibilities of MoH, NMS, and JMS, and how to verify medicine consignments by checking information such as batch numbers, expiry dates, dosage forms, and units of measure.

Both MoH and NMS were strategic partners from a policy perspective, able to leverage the findings to inform ongoing policy debates, as well as incorporate recommendations in midterm review processes. Their participation also contributed legitimacy and credibility to the entire exercise.

UNHCO and HEPS had wide recognition at the community level and broad experience leading citizen-oriented monitoring activities linked to access to medicines and health service delivery. Both organizations had just completed a client satisfaction survey (UNHCO and HEPS 2012), which was well received and may have, in part, laid the groundwork for the more extensive exercise envisioned by the coalition. UNHCO also had strong links with community groups nationwide and could more easily deploy its partners to conduct data collection in remote areas, reducing costs, and leveraging district-level capacity to conduct the surveys.

Given UNHCO's track record in designing and administering field surveys, the CSO group was given primary oversight of the data collection exercise. This role would be shared with AFIC, which was viewed as having a comparative advantage in performing rigorous data analysis.

Collectively, the team shared responsibility for designing the study protocol, data collection methods, analytical framework, field test plan, sampling design, data collectors training manual, and field operational plan. Stakeholders also volunteered for specific roles such as coordination and logistics (UNHCO), central technical team leadership (JMS), and field supervision (MoH, NMS, HEPS). The roles and responsibilities of each team member were articulated through Terms of Reference.

In order to sustain team cohesion and avoid tensions over the emerging findings of the data collection exercise, it was important to reinforce repeatedly the collective benefits derived from the initiative. Team members were also encouraged to discuss their concerns and any emerging issues openly, and norms were established to ensure democratic decision-making processes. It was critical that the team accepted ownership and responsibility for all of the findings—both positive and negative—that emerged from the data collection exercise. Emphasis was given to focusing on understanding the sector challenges so that the coalition would be better placed to help address them as a collective. This way, "blaming and shaming" of partners was strongly discouraged. The process of creating a safe environment where all actors felt protected during the data gathering proved one of the most difficult challenges. However, without team cohesion and a sense of a shared mission and trust, it would have been virtually impossible to embark on an activity as sensitive as data gathering on contentious issues.

Validating the Data

In May 2013, MeTA Uganda successfully collected data from 10 districts (see table 4.1; representing 10 percent of all districts), 200 households, 202 health facilities, 20 focus groups, 3,040 patients, and 486 key informants. This represented one of the most comprehensive data collection exercises conducted collectively by Uganda's public and private sectors and civil society. (See appendix E for summary of findings and infographic.)

To secure broad buy-in and mitigate the risks of the data being rejected by different stakeholder groups, MeTA Uganda organized a validation meeting where it explained the study rationale, the findings, and proposed recommendations. While this meeting exposed some of the tensions between agencies, in general the findings were broadly accepted. It was agreed that stakeholders would work together to address the emerging issues, rather than place blame on specific agencies. Such an approach would prove more constructive both in the short and longterm.

An additional opportunity to validate the findings of the data collection came through a strategic partnership with UNICEF, which allowed MeTA Uganda to leverage existing short message service (SMS)-based technologies (e.g., texting) called *mTrac* and *U-report*, directly linked to the MoH's Resource Centre.[7] Through mTrac, health facility workers can send government reports by SMS, including real-time data, to map facility stocks with the aim of avoiding stock-outs and ensuring transparency and accountability for drug supplies. U-report is a user-centered social monitoring tool based on simple SMS messages (including poll

Table 4.1 Assignments for District Data Collection

Team leader	Districts	Supervisor
Africa Freedom of Information Center (AFIC) Uganda National Health Consumers/Users' Organization (UNHCO)	**WAKISO**	UNHCO
Uganda Debt Network (UDN)	**MBARARA**	WACSO
UNHCO	**NWOYA**	UNHCO
Coalition for Health Promotion and Social Development (HEPS)	**PALLISA**	Pallisa Civil Society Organizations' Network (PACONET)
Ministry of Health (MOH)	**KASESE**	Kabarole Research & Resource Center (KRC)
Action Group for Health Human Rights and HIV/AIDS (AGHA)	**NEBBI**	NEBBI NGO FORUM
National Medical Stores (NMS)	**OYAM**	UNHCO
UNHCO	**SOROTI**	Mama's Club
UNHCO	**KAPCHORWA**	KACSO
Joint Medical Store (JMS)	**IGANGA**	UNHCO

Source: MeTA 2014.
Note: Table shows the division of labor and responsibilities by district for the data collection exercise. In the spirit of collaboration, this was done to involve as many MeTA members as could undertake the task.

questions and survey results) and designed to strengthen community-led development and citizen engagement. Leveraging this strategic relationship, MeTA Uganda worked closely with UNICEF to translate the survey questionnaire used in the field into short text that could be sent via SMS. This was then deployed through the U-report and mTrac platforms to gather data on client satisfaction with service delivery and challenges associated with pharmaceutical PSM.

The impact these tools had on MeTA's data collection can be summarized as reach, speed, and cost efficiency. Through these technologies, the coalition had access to more than 16,000 Ugandans (three times the number of citizens surveyed at community level using traditional survey instruments) and 2,100 health facilities (10 times the number of facilities surveyed through traditional channels). It could poll these in a matter of minutes, for less than two US cents per-SMS message. Achieving such reach at such speed with very little cost was a step forward for the coalition. Within the context of the data collection exercise, these technologies supplied a rapid and cost-effective way to map general sentiments on specific issues, further enabling the coalition to fine-tune the findings of its data collection, as well as to gain increased visibility for its work.

A Strong Initial Impact

MeTA Uganda disseminated its findings at a high-level policy workshop in February 2014. Chaired by MoH, it raised important issues about the efficacy of reforms, notably the delivery of medicines to health facilities, and the role of local government authorities and CSOs in better monitoring health service delivery. In terms of impact, the study accelerated a review of NMS delivery schedules and has prompted appropriate changes and modifications. Other outcomes include the following:

1. The findings of the study fed into the midterm review of HSSIP II, as well as the Annual Health Sector Report (2012–13), providing an important evidence base for policy debate.
2. Civil society actors were trained in 10 districts nationwide and can, on a periodic basis, collect data on health service delivery, citizen empowerment, and medicine availability.
3. A national baseline was established around the three main areas of focus, from which reform efforts can be measured over time and assessed. These three main areas of focus are client satisfaction with health service delivery in public facilities, the availability of medicines in health facilities, and levels of citizen empowerment in advocating better service delivery at health facilities.
4. New tools were created that can be used and customized not only by members of the coalition but also by global practitioners through an online community of practice.
5. Coalition actors developed and demonstrated their capacity to work together on a discreet initiative, to surmount traditional barriers to collaboration and to take joint ownership for system failures and for catalyzing reforms.

Lessons Learned

Based on the experiences of working together to achieve a common objective, MeTA Uganda drew several key lessons, as outlined in box 4.1.

Box 4.1 Key Lessons in the Establishment of a Multistakeholder Group: Uganda

1. Maintaining cohesion—Multistakeholder coalitions present many advantages, but also pose several challenges. The major advantages are the diversity of knowledge, resources, ideas, and tools contributed by members, as well as the strategic partnerships formed. Nevertheless, as is natural in any grouping of varying interests, tensions are bound to exist. To manage these tensions, it is important to recognize existing sensitivities and to make every effort to address concerns, as well as to mitigate potential conflicts. In this regard, there is a clear role for the coalition leadership (the national convener) to communicate effectively with members, constantly clarify goals and objectives, and set clear expectations.

   Multistakeholder coalitions are more likely to be effective when they create changes in both demand- and supply-side behaviors. It is the "sum of the parts" rather than the individual capabilities that enhance the quality, strength, and cohesion of the coalition. Actors must therefore view themselves as a unified force, working toward a shared goal. This will give interventions more traction in areas collectively viewed as important.

2. Demonstrating credibility—Multistakeholder interventions seem to have greater prospect for success in places where the national conveners are seen as authoritative, legitimate, and credible. MeTA Uganda was fortunate to have both global support—through the UK's Department for International Development, WHO, HAI Africa, and the World Bank—and domestic support through MoH. It also demonstrated competency and capacity through high-level studies and community-led interventions endorsed by a variety of stakeholders.

3. Mobilizing high-level commitment—High-level commitment is integral to coalition success, particularly if the objective of the group is to accelerate the reform agenda. MeTA Uganda found that while representatives of the various agencies sat on its council, it was also important that high-level policymakers were aware of its activities, endorsed them, and provided the space for MeTA's input into policy reforms. It helped that members of the council also participated in other forums, convened by the ministry, through which the coalition could advance its agenda.

4. Roadblocks can be a pathway to innovate—The best laid plans often go awry. It is important to recognize that there is no standard roadmap or series of steps guaranteed to ensure success. Rather, coalitions have to view the process of collective action as one requiring the ability to adapt to evolving realities on the ground, as well as a process that is context driven. An approach to coalition building or tackling a particular issue that may work in Kenya would not necessarily be relevant in Uganda. Acknowledging these differences allows coalitions to be more flexible when faced with emerging challenges and obstacles, and better prepared to innovate.

---

box continues next page

Box 4.1 Key Lessons in the Establishment of a Multistakeholder Group: Uganda *(continued)*

5. Respect for stakeholder sensitivities—When working with stakeholders, it is important to nuance language in order to prevent "putting them off". Words like "corruption," for instance, tend to elicit defensive responses from government. Rather, it is important to emphasize cooperation, collaboration, and partnership, words that suggest *working together,* rather than accusation or blame—but also working together to address emerging challenges for a common objective, as opposed to pointing fingers. A high premium should also be placed on diplomacy as well tact in presenting potentially negative or controversial issues. When success is achieved by any partner, it is always important to celebrate together and give credit to the collaboration.

6. Celebrating individualism and independence—One of the biggest fears in the coalition is the possibility of "being swallowed up" or "losing identity". There will be members who are outspoken and others who may feel left out. Cohesion depends on being accommodating and on the leadership reaching out to members who may not be as imposing as others. A level playing field should be created so that everybody feels empowered to participate and maintain independence.

7. What's in it for me?—A partnership is considered successful, and will be sustainable, only if all members are satisfied that the benefits are worth the investment. This is particularly true for the private sector. It is important to keep checking and ensuring that everybody is happy and committed.

Notes

1. Last-mile delivery is the only link in the supply chain that directly touches the customer.

2. The Flagship Framework comprises a set of analytical tools that are combined into an overall, structured methodology for developing, adapting, and implementing reform proposals. It also includes a comprehensive review of reform alternatives and a systematic review of their strengths and weaknesses in various situations. It is helpful for developing reform proposals and has been used by a number of countries to analyze their situations and develop reform plans. Roberts, Marc J. and Reich, Michael J. 2011. *Pharmaceutical Reform: A Guide to Improving Performance and Equity.* Washington, DC: World Bank.

3. The Rapid Results Approach is a methodology that empowers teams to achieve results quickly—in 100 days. It is also a way of approaching bringing about large-scale change step-by-step through smaller initiatives.

4. A highlight of the workshop was the launch of the online community of practice, http://www.enepp.net.

5. WHO defines E-health as the transfer of health resources and health care by electronic means. It encompasses three main areas: The delivery of health information, for health professionals and health consumers, through the Internet and telecommunications; Using the power of IT and e-commerce to improve public health services—for example, through the education and training of health workers; and the use of e-commerce and e-business practices in health systems management. See http://www.who.int/trade/glossary/story021/en/ (accessed June 24, 2014).

6. The Global Observatory for eHealth (GOe) defines mHealth or mobile health as medical and public health practice supported by mobile devices, such as mobile phones, patient monitoring devices, personal digital assistants (PDAs), and other wireless devices. See Global Observatory for eHealth series—Volume 3, 2011 available at http://www.who.int/goe/publications/goe_mhealth_web.pdf (accessed June 24, 2014).

7. The MOH Resource Centre was established by the Ministry of Health in 1999 with the mandate "to develop an enabling environment for, and undertake activities to support, effective and efficient management of information of the entire health sector", in collaboration with existing information services (for example, local government and others). The overall goal of the center is to establish and maintain a comprehensive source of routine health information for planning, implementation, and evaluation of health care. See http://health.go.ug/mohweb/?page_id=396 (accessed June 16, 2014).

CHAPTER 5

Epilogue

In the last four years, the World Bank Institute (WBI) has accelerated the formation of multistakeholder coalitions in Kenya, Tanzania, and Uganda. Working closely with actors in the public sector, private sector, and civil society, WBI has helped to transition these stakeholders from disparate groups working in silos to multisectoral groupings working *together* toward the attainment of shared objectives. While each coalition has had to face many challenges along the way, they have also succeeded in achieving important milestones. These early successes have not only strengthened the coalitions, but have also demonstrated the potential for collective action—when sustained and nurtured—to catalyze reform processes. This epilogue provides an important summary of the major achievements made and looks ahead at what the future holds for the coalitions.

Kenya: The Forum for Transparency and Accountability in Pharmaceutical Procurement

In May 2013, the Kenya Forum for Transparency and Accountability in Pharmaceutical Procurement (FoTAPP) conducted a survey intended to gather data on: (1) citizens' and health providers' satisfaction with health service delivery; and (2) the availability of essential medicines at the health facility level. As the Ministry of Health, a member of the coalition was also—at the time—implementing several social accountability interventions at the facility level, the survey also provided an opportunity to track progress on these efforts. The coalition collected data from 20 facilities (including nine pilot sites of the MoH project), which represented nine counties.

The data collection exercise, along with stakeholder consultations to discuss issues and recommendations, enabled the coalition to gain both visibility and credibility in policy dialogues around social accountability in the health sector. As a result, Transparency International (TI) Kenya[1]—the convener of FoTAPP— is now a permanent CSO representative on the Ministry of Health's Technical

Working Group for Social Accountability. Furthermore, the organization has contributed to the development of the Ministry of Health's new Social Accountability manual. FoTAPP—at the request of the sector—has also provided substantive comments and recommendations on the Draft Health Bill. In this vein, the coalition—in accordance with its goal for greater openness and inclusiveness in the sector—has provided recommendations on how to better incorporate the principles of transparency, accountability and citizen participation in the Bill. These principles are also viewed as critical to realizing the constitutional Right to Health and efficiency in the health sector as a whole. Through donor support,[2] TI Kenya will also be scaling up the Mobile Drug Tracking System[3] (MDTS) to include a web-based portal where citizens can readily access information on medicine availability at health facilities nationwide. The portal will also include a Medicines Price Reference Guide, intended to enhance transparency in the procurement of medicines, especially within the context of Kenya's newly devolved health system, where several suppliers will compete for business at the county level rather than at the central level. The MDTS has also been adapted for use in other sectors beyond health, notably in education.

Tanzania: The Tanzania Multistakeholder Group on Pharmaceutical Procurement

In Tanzania, the coalition has completed a regional procurement monitoring exercise in all six districts of Dodoma. In this exercise, the coalition worked closely with the Public Procurement and Regulatory Authority to monitor the region's compliance with the Public Procurement Act, as well as to determine the capacity and performance of the pharmaceutical supply chain. The exercise was aimed at piloting tools and procedures that could be implemented throughout the country to observe technical aspects of the pharmaceutical procurement and supply chain. The pilot was conducted in Dodoma because it addresses downstream activities of a complementary donor-supported project on health system strengthening also being undertaken in Dodoma. The coalition also conducted a stock monitoring exercise of selected tracer medicines at district hospitals in the region. As a direct follow-up to this work, the coalition is exploring scaling up to other districts in partnership with donors who have expressed an interest in building on the coalition's pioneering efforts.

Uganda: The Medicines Transparency Alliance

In Uganda, following the dissemination of the coalition's report on *Client Satisfaction with Services in Uganda's Public Health Facilities*, the National Medical Stores (NMS) and the Ministry of Health have initiated remedial actions intended to address some of the emerging issues. The NMS, for instance, is reevaluating its delivery schedules with a view to improving the last mile distribution of lifesaving medicines. The work of MeTA Uganda has strengthened its relationship and partnership with the Ministry of Health, beyond the Pharmaceutical Department. Specifically, the success of the data collection served as a critical illustration of the potential for state and non-state actors to track reforms in the health sector. Consequently, the coalition—under the auspices of the Uganda Health Systems Strengthening Project (UHSSP)—is carrying out an extensive monitoring initiative to track progress in the implementation of certain components of the Health Sector Strategic Investment Plan. Specifically, the coalition—represented by the Uganda National Health Consumers'/Users' Organization—will pilot an ICT-enabled community scorecard and client satisfaction survey in two districts, in order to obtain citizen feedback on health service delivery with a focus on reform areas. Furthermore, it will also monitor the reporting of maternal and perinatal deaths at the facility level. Additionally, the coalition will complement the facilities' routine reporting with a community-focused system—managed by Village Health Teams—that reports on deaths occurring *outside* the facility. The coalition will also continue to routinely monitor medicine stockouts at health facilities to complement the ongoing reforms led by the Ministry, the NMS and the Joint Medical Stores.

Looking Ahead

After nearly five years of building coalitions—from scratch—to advance reforms in the health sector, actors are beginning to appreciate the value of working collectively. While there has always been an understanding of the importance of collaboration, stakeholders now have the tools, the evidence base, and the experience necessary to facilitate cooperation and joint interventions.

The coalition building approach, however, does not present a panacea, but rather presents a complementary approach to solving complex challenges in the health sector. Transformative change in the sector will require an iterative process of trial and error. If sustained and nurtured, coalitions could begin to unlock some of the difficult challenges facing the sector and help countries potentially realize goals such as Universal Health Coverage at a quicker pace.

The next few years are going to be critical for the coalitions in East Africa. To be successful, actors will need to leverage their knowledge and experiences—in working collectively—to set in motion reform processes that are deep-rooted in shared goals for tangible advancements in health service delivery. It is not only important to focus on incremental achievements and milestones, but also to develop mechanisms for distilling and sharing insights on "what works". In that regard, the authors view this book as only one step toward a longer-term effort of experimentation and learning. We therefore invite practitioners to share their experiences and to explore ways of adding to the knowledge on the impact of collective action in accelerating reforms.

Notes

1. TI Kenya is leading on many of the coalition's follow-up activities for three main reasons: It serves as the national convener for the coalition and is thus mandated to lead all coordination and implementation of activities; as FoTAPP is not a legal entity, it cannot receive funds from donors or other sources, hence, TI Kenya serves as a secretariat for channeling resources intended to support coalition activities; the coalition's activities are closely aligned with some of TI Kenya's existing programs, thereby making it easier to leverage the organization's own resources—such as staff, transport vehicles, stationery—to support coalition activities.

2. The global consortium Making All Voices Count (http://www.makingallvoicescount. org/), has awarded Transparency International Kenya—as convener of FoTAPP—140,000 GBP to scale up the MDTS and develop the Medicines Price Reference Guide.

3. The MDTS was designed and piloted by FoTAPP in close collaboration with the Kenya Medical Supplies Authority in 2012.

Using a Multi-Stakeholder Approach to Improve Governance in Pharmaceutical Procurement

Implementation Progress: Uganda, Kenya, Tanzania

According to the European Health Care Fraud and Corruption Network and the World Health Organization, annual global health expenditure stands at about US$ 5.3 trillion. Of this outlay, US$ 750 billion (18%) is spent in the pharmaceutical market (World Health Organization [WHO] 2013), while consumers lose about US$ 300 billion more to human error and corruption (European Healthcare Fraud and Corruption Network 2010). Together, total expenditure for pharmaceuticals and corruption combined exceeds US$ 1 trillion, or approximately 1/5th of what is spent globally on health care.

Pharmaceutical procurement is particularly prone to poor governance, as it entails complex processes which involve many stakeholders, including government ministries, manufacturers, hospitals, and other distributors. When pharmaceutical procurement and supply chain systems work effectively, they offer high levels of quality, cost-effectiveness, product availability, transparency, accountability, and value for money in the use of public funds.

The effort to improve these systems is especially critical in emerging markets, where pharmaceutical spending is 20–30% higher than the global average (Lu et al. 2010). International reference prices and cross-country knowledge-sharing are thus critical to low-income countries obtaining fair prices on the global pharmaceutical market.

As part of the drive to increase resource efficiency and improve health outcomes through better governance in pharmaceutical markets, the World Bank Institute (WBI) has initiated a multi-year capacity-building initiative which will bring multiple stakeholders involved in the procurement process to forge consensus on governance challenges, identify areas for action and improvement, initiate peer-to-peer learning, and facilitate the implementation of measures to improve transparency and accountability in pharmaceutical procurement.

The initiative targets three countries in Africa—Tanzania, Kenya, and Uganda. These countries make excellent candidates for this program as they have been leaders in reforming pharmaceutical procurement processes and they possess the capacity to further capitalize on these reforms through knowledge exchange and further policy action. The initiative focuses on five main dimensions of governance: (i) Legal and regulatory framework; (ii) Poor quantification; (iii) Process gaps; (iv) Institutional arrangement; and (v) Disclosure of information. Corruption is implicit in each category as a symptom, factor, or cause of poor governance.

The initiative has recently entered its final Phase, Phase IV. This document briefly describes the initiative's progress thus far.

PHASE I

Objective: Determine governance issues and build consensus among stakeholders at the country level

Phase I leveraged a multi-pronged approach to understanding the strengths and weaknesses of the procurement processes in each country through four activities: a desk review, consultations with key informants, a benchmarking assessment of each country's Medicines Procurement Agency, and an in-country validation meeting. This effort brought together diverse stakeholders with procurement and policy expertise from the public and private sectors, civil society organizations, development partners, and academia.

Desk Review and Informant Interviews: Phase I began in January 2010 with a rigorous desk review of literature from each country. WBI gathered this literature from key informants, development partners, references and footnotes from relevant documents, unpublished "gray" literature, and electronic research. Following the desk review, WBI conducted interviews with a number of stakeholders from each country using a unique tool which was tailored to gather knowledge on the procurement process. The tool is distinct from the standard WHO tool for measuring transparency and governance in pharmaceutical procurement in three ways: (i) WBI tailored the questionnaire to procurement, rather than generalizing the questionnaire to the entire supply chain; (ii) the tool delves more deeply into procurement practices and procurement-related activities, as it contains a greater number of questions; and (iii) the questionnaire employs a more open-ended approach, using questions that describe situations and practices instead of questions that garner yes/no responses. The questionnaire contains 51 questions on the procurement process, most of which incorporate sub-questions.

Benchmarking Exercise: WBI built upon knowledge gathered from the interviews with a systematic benchmarking exercise that assessed the standard operating procedures, organizational structure, institutional capacity, and functioning of each country's Medicines Procurement Agency. The tool used a 170-point questionnaire which probed nine dimensions of procurement-related governance, rating compliance on a scale of 0 to 3; the dimensions included Agency Resources (mainly IT and personnel), Procedures and Processes within the Procurement Cycle (the advertisement and evaluation of bids, the use of pre and post-qualification, contract award and administration, etc), Transparency (processes, records handling, etc), Support and Control Systems (internal and external audits), Record Keeping (semi-annual and annual reports detailing bidding process and contract administration), Risk Assessment (corruption and compliance control), Assessment by Private Sector Suppliers (transparency and accountability), and Regional Collaboration and Information Sharing (pricing, practice, and peer-review).

Validation Workshops: This groundwork culminated with a meeting of stakeholders in each country to validate the findings of the Phase I research, seek consensus on the most critical areas for improvement, prioritize areas in which to take action, and draft a country report detailing the Initiative's findings from Phase I. The meetings, which took place in October and November of 2010, were productive and lively: each brought together nearly 20 participants from government agencies, academia, the donor community, and other experts who represent significant stakeholder groups or who had participated in the Phase I interview process. The country teams validated initial research findings: that the legal and regulatory frameworks, procurement monitoring, contract management, disclosure of information, and quantification were some of the challenges facing stakeholders in participating countries.

The careful research gleaned from each stage of Phase I provided a clear picture of each country's procurement system, as well as the mechanisms in place to ensure transparency and accountability in each, the extent to which these mechanisms are used, and their levels of effectiveness. Phase I analyses also assessed procedural gaps and challenges in procurement, country-wide efforts to improve pharmaceutical procurement practice, and the good practices each country currently employs.

What We've Learned: Common Challenges and Best Practices in Each Country

GENERAL OBSERVATIONS

- Major efforts are already underway to upgrade pharmaceutical procurement procedures in each country, either through the restructuring of medicines procurement agencies, legal reform, or technical training.

- There is a great need for regional collaboration and information-sharing: this was consistently the weakest dimension for each country, according to the results of the Benchmarking Exercise.

- There are legal and regulatory foundations framing pharmaceutical procurement in each country, but implementation remains a challenge.

- Moving forward, all countries generally prioritized collaboration amongst multiple stake-holders and capacity-building as the main focus for action.

COUNTRY-SPECIFIC CHALLENGES AND BEST PRACTICES

In Tanzania

- *Challenges* include weak civil society involvement, a surfeit of quantification tools and methods, weak coordination in procurement planning, lack of accountability mechanisms, poor disclosure of information, and capacity constraints at the national and decentralized levels, and necessary improvements to the legal and regulatory structures surrounding procurement. The country has prioritized several areas for action, including national-level quantification and procurement planning, facility-level quantification, the role of CSOs in the interaction between providers and end-users, human resources development and deployment, multi-stakeholder relations (especially public-private partnerships), regional collaboration and sharing of information, private sector supplier assessment, and the improvement of general risk assessment methodologies.

- *Best practices* include Tanzania's Public Procurement Act of 2004, which is a successful working model for decentralized public sector procurement, supported by a strong Public Procurement Regulatory Authority that has carried out very effective training for procurement entities. Other strengths include the examples Tanzania's Medical Stores Department (MSD) Procurement Management Unit (PMU), which exemplifies a number of best practices, including the Contract Management Flow Chart, which acts as a useful guide to contract management, and the Vendor Rating Tool, which provides an unbiased way of recording and rating vendor performance to ensure that inefficient and unreliable suppliers are identified and avoided in future transactions. Finally, MSD's planned use of the Enterprise Resource Program (ERP) will be a ground-breaking initiative from which other procurement professionals can learn.

In Kenya

- *Challenges* include the need for more coordination among the civil society organizations (CSOs) working in this area. Even though there are well-established institutions and regulations to guide procurement, their practical implementation and adherence is not well-coordinated. Coordination could perhaps be improved by increasing the transparency of information to ensure efficiency and compliance to regulation; specifically, making the post-bid opening stage of procurement information formally and officially accessible would increase transparency. Other challenges that remain include delays in pharmaceutical delivery, product stock-outs, and insufficient quantities of essential medicines. Finally, KEMSA continues to lack independence with respect to budget expenditure.

- *Best practices* include well-established institutions and regulations to guide Kenya Medical Supplies Agency (KEMSA) to efficiently purchase, receive, store, manage and distribute pharmaceuticals and health products. The institutional configuration within the pharmaceutical sector is also notable in Kenya. Other strengths include the vibrant array of CSOs in Kenya, such as HAI Africa, which support improved health outcomes through pharmaceuticals in their mission to promote access to and safe use of essential medicines in Kenya. Furthermore, Kenya has made strides to reform the legal framework regulating pharmaceutical procurement, efforts which include the revision of Chapter 244 of the Pharmacy and Poisons Act, the establishment of The Public Procurement Oversight Authority, the reorganization of the Kenya Medical Supplies Agency, and the reworking of both the Kenya Essential Medicines List (KEML) and the Standard Treatment Guidelines (STG) in June of 2010.

In Uganda

- *Challenges* include the failure of practitioners to effectively apply the provisions of the procurement law in procurement of medicines, weak coordination between the government agencies involved in the procurement process, and supply chain management gaps. Additionally, public sector procurement is burdened by an overly-bureaucratic system which has not yet successfully operationalized procurement law. Remaining process gaps include the transparency of contract and supply chain management, the cumbersome nature of the appeals process, the procedures and regulations surrounding accountability mechanisms and audits, the need for inter-departmental coordination between governmental agencies regulating procurement, and the process by which information on procurement is disclosed.

- *Best practices* include successful multi-stakeholder collaboration through Medicines Transparency Alliance Uganda (MeTA); MeTA has used collaboration and discourse to promote cross-sectoral information sharing, the disclosure of information on volumes and values of medicines imported into Uganda, and pursued the amendment of the Procurement Act and Anti-Counterfeit Goods Bill. Other strengths include the participation of CSOs such as The Coalition for Health Promotion and Social Development (HEPS), which promote increased access to affordable essential medicines through advocacy. Additionally, the establishment of several key pieces of legislation passed in the last decade is also noteworthy; this includes the passage of the National Medicines Policy and the Public Procurement and Disposal of Public Assets Act. Other best practices include the release of information regarding the results of bidding processes on the part of NMS, and Uganda's efforts to collaborate with other regional partners.

PHASE II

Implementing What We've Learned Round Table: On February 24, 2011, the Initiative convened a Round Table Meeting on "Using a Multi-Stakeholder Approach to Improve Governance in Pharmaceutical Procurement;" the Round Table brought together policy makers, representatives from government, civil society organizations, international development agencies (including the World Bank), academia, and other major players to engage in dialogue and offer responses and critiques to WBI's Initiative. The Round Table offered participating policy-makers and practitioners an opportunity to forge new alliances and investigate collaborative strategies to propel the Initiative forward in its mission to strengthen and institutionalize accountability and transparency in pharmaceutical procurement. The day's discussions gained a new dimension following the presentation by the Asociación Nacional de Empresarios de Colombia, which demonstrated the requirements for creating a successful multi-stakeholder platform, a major end-goal of WBI's Initiative. This diverse group engendered a lively and insightful discussion, and produced a wealth of ideas to propel the Initiative forward and carefully examine health delivery systems in an integrated manner.

Regional Workshop (Nairobi): The Initiative continued to add momentum to the dialogue that the Round Table generated through a regional knowledge-sharing workshop, held in April 2011 in Nairobi, on the topic of "Pharmaceutical Procurement and Governance in East Africa." The workshop brought together 51 key stakeholders from Tanzania, Kenya, and Uganda to engage in "collective action learning," a process which involves interactive knowledge-sharing and exchange, reflection, and action planning—crucial steps toward solving many of the thorny, obstinate issues surrounding pharmaceutical procurement, which have been able to flourish due to a lack of transparency and dialogue.

The workshop objectives converged around stimulating collective action to promote accountability, transparency, and sustainability in pharmaceutical procurement processes; they included (i) Creating multi-stakeholder country coalitions committed to improving the governance (transparency & accountability) of procurement and supply chain management (PSM) of pharmaceuticals in Kenya, Tanzania and Uganda; (ii) Assembling draft action plans for strengthening transparency and accountability in pharmaceutical procurement; and (iii) Bringing together a regional network and introducing and launching an e-platform to facilitate peer-to-peer learning.

Over the course of the workshop, participating stakeholders were introduced to a wealth of tools, topics, and approaches to develop robust and transparent pharmaceutical governance processes through workshop presentations and plenary discussions. These sessions allowed country teams to discuss their unmet needs, diagnose pressing problems in procurement, and draft country action plans that address procurement issues within their country.

The workshop presented participants with a valuable opportunity to share a wealth of experience and learn from one another. The invaluable nature of this learning experience was reflected by participants in anonymous evaluations, which were tremendously positive. In the evaluations, participants highlighted the relevance and usefulness of the discussions and presentations by workshop facilitators, with especially high ratings for each. There was strong agreement that the workshop objectives had been met and collaboration with WBI in the future would be an essential element in galvanizing change in pharmaceutical procurement.

Electronic Platform to Host the Network of Procurement Practitioners (e-NePP): The Nairobi Workshop included the exciting and much-anticipated launch of E-nepp, an electronic information-sharing and capacity-building tool for procurement practitioners. Since the platform's launch, over 100 procurement professionals have registered, 3 country groups had been formed (Kenya, Tanzania and Uganda), and a vibrant, ongoing dialogue that started with the workshop has continued on the platform.

The platform includes relevant and useful documentation for practitioners and policy-makers, such as texts and presentations from the Workshop, as well as medicines price information data for the 3 participating countries. In the longer-term, the price data will be extended to also include price information from the private sector procuring for faith-based organizations. The access to comparative price information could help procurement agencies better negotiate contracts and ensure competitive prices as well as share information on supplier performance. At the same time, it will enable civil society groups to have a better sense of market prices to more effectively monitor the sale and distribution of these products.

Action Plan Progress: Each of the participating countries has already made strong headway with their respective Action Plans. Issues common to all three countries include: (i) the legal status of their multi-stakeholder groups (ii) the training of CSOs to build capacity and (iii) developing an ICT Platform.

Tanzania: The country has developed an action plan, with concrete implementation steps, for the following 3 activities at the country level: (i) strengthen multi-stakeholder coalitions (ii) empower CSOs in good governance and (iii) employ mobile tracking technology.

Uganda: The following 2 activities will be implemented as part of Uganda's Action Plan to improve the quality and availability of medicines: (i) engage multi-stakeholder groups through a debriefing meeting and (ii) operationalize project team management of draft concept notes on (i) building CSO capacity and (ii) improving information flow. Additionally, the Ministry is including the ICT project in its work program and final year work plans.

Kenya: Kenya will implement the following 3 activities as part of its Action Plan: (i) establish a multi-stakeholder group with a clear mandate (ii) agree on roles and responsibilities and

(iii) identify projects and project teams. For the first quarter, project teams have been identified for the following areas: (i) ICT (ii) governance and (iii) public education.

Training of Trainers (ToT) Manual: The MSGs—with support from the World Bank Institute has developed a Training of Trainers Manual for civil society organizations (CSO). This manual is a first step toward equipping CSOs with the necessary tools to more effectively monitor pharmaceutical PSM processes. The manual is a training guide and a "living document" that can be updated as experiences are acquired and lessons learned. Its design facilitates adaptation to a variety of sectors and settings.

Training of Trainers Workshop: In December 2011, the World Bank Institute hosted forty representatives of CSOs from all three countries, at a regional Training of Trainers (ToT) Workshop, held in Dar es Salaam, Tanzania. The objective of the workshop was to review the fundamental principles of pharmaceutical procurement and supply chain management (PSM), as well as train these CSO representatives on the use of social accountability tools in monitoring PSM practices, procedures, and processes. Workshop participants also reviewed a draft of the ToT manual and provided feedback for its finalization. The manual has been finalized, and as of July 1, will become available as an online resource.

'Quick Win' Projects: In February 2012, the World Bank Institute provided resources to the multistakeholder coalitions. This funding is intended to support short-term, high-impact projects, called 'Quick Win' projects. These Quick Win activities will help catalyze the implementation of the country action plans, developed by the multistakeholder coalitions in April 2011. Through the WBI funding, the coalitions have initiated critical activities around three main areas: CSO empowerment through training on PSM; the use of ICT in monitoring medicine availability in health facilities; and research and analysis on gaps in PSM processes at the country level. All these activities will be completed by June 30; findings from these initial activities will help inform the scale-up of longer-term coalition activities and the mobilization of resources to support such expansion moving forward.

Regional Workshop (Kampala): In April 2012, the World Bank Institute hosted its third regional workshop in Uganda, Kampala. The theme of the workshop was *"Strengthening Multistakeholder Coalitions through Leadership Action'.* Its objective was to: (i) examine multistakeholder group progress in implementing their country action plans; and (ii) provide a structured leadership course tailored towards providing specific tools to enable the coalitions better overcome implementation challenges. Over the course of 5 days, the workshop participants acquired tools around Adaptive Leadership, Strategic Communication & Negotiation, Coalition Building, Rapid Results Approaches, and Self Mastery. The insights form these courses provided critical frameworks for developing reprioritized action plans, with 100-day milestones. The reprioritized action plans underscored the importance of continuing activities around CSO empowerment and data collection. The workshop also led to a renewed focus on strengthening relationships with government.

High Level Policy Makers' Meeting: During the April 2012 workshop, WBI also hosted a one-day high-level policy makers meeting. The objective of the meeting was to explore strategies for better integrating the multistakeholder coalitions in national PSM reform efforts. The meeting, attended by 11 senior ranking officials from ministries of health, procurement agencies, and faith-based organizations, underscored the importance of collaboration and also emphasized the role that multistakeholder coalitions can play in serving as a critical bridge between government and the citizens. Through this meeting, government officials committed to more active participation in the multistakeholder coalitions and identified tangible opportunities for engagement, particularly around the use of mobile technology in enhancing citizen feedback mechanisms on the effectiveness of PSM. Since the meeting, both the coalitions in Kenya and Tanzania have partnered with the Kenya Medicines Supplies Agency (KEMSA) and the Tanzania Public Procurement Regulatory Authority respectively. In Kenya, the partners are rolling out a mobile system for tracking medicine availability and in Tanzania; they are training CSOs on the use of selected tools to monitor PSM processes in pilot sites across the country.

PHASE III

Capacity Building: The April 2012 WBI regional multistakeholder meeting in Kampala identified critical capacity gaps in addressing communication challenges in procurement and supply chain management reforms. To address this capacity constraint, the coalitions requested WBI technical assistance to develop country specific communication strategies. These communication strategies will help the coalitions to: (i) better identify sources of external support; (ii) recognize and address opposition to reform and; (iii) proactively engage different stakeholders to understand the underlying interests that can be tapped for supporting reforms and increase collaboration.

In May 2013, WBI sponsored workshops in Kenya and Uganda to discuss, develop, and finalize communication strategies for FoTAPP and MeTA respectively. FoTAPP's communication objective is "To increase citizen participation in using Mobile Drug Tracking System (MDTS) in tracking the pharmaceutical commodities at Level III health facility." MeTA's communication strategy aims: "To create broad based understanding of the 'crisis' of ineffective and wasteful health service delivery at the facility level and mobilize both 'supply-side' and 'demand-side' actors to address implementation hurdles."

Data Collection Tools: In October 2012, a regional team of experts representing government and civil society from Kenya, Tanzania and Uganda refined, standardized, and finalized data collection tools developed and pre-tested by the coalitions. The technical working group of experts also developed a monitoring and evaluation framework to guide the refinement, finalization and rollout of the tools. They identified the need for two supplementary data collection tools: a Citizen Empowerment Tool to determine the existence of and assess the efficacy of Grievance Redress Mechanisms in receiving and responding to citizen feedback on health service delivery, as well as a Stock Monitoring Tool to track stock levels of tracer medicines in selected health facilities in all three countries. The set of harmonized tools will aid cross-country comparison and analyses to gain a broader picture of citizen satisfaction with health services, access to medicines and citizen empowerment across the region.

WBI facilitated the technical working group meeting to refine, standardize and finalize the data collection tools, as well as develop supplementary tools and outline an appropriate M&E framework.

Surveys: Also in October 2012, the Multi-stakeholder Group on Pharmaceutical Procurement in Tanzania conducted a procurement and stock monitoring exercise in all six districts of the Dodoma region. The study found that all districts have procurement structures in place, but revealed wide variations in pharmaceutical procurement activities, including:

- Some districts' human resource capacity is compromised by leave granted to procurement staff.
- Only one district (Chamwino) floats tenders for pharmaceutical supplies.
- 'Shopping' (procurement by quotation) is the most common method of procurement for items not available at the national Medical Stores Department (MSD).
- All districts had fair levels of 28 tracer medicines in stock, although Bahi and Dodoma Municipality had stock levels of less than 80 percent for these items. At the regional level, only 32 percent of tracer items were available in *all* district hospitals at the time of the monitoring exercise.
- Procurement from non-MSD sources has an important cushioning effect on stock levels.

Tanzania's survey tools could also be used to assess the quality of medicines in stock (such as their source, batch numbers and expiry dates), which will help curb the circulation of counterfeit medicines.

In Kenya, the overall goal of FoTAPP's survey, carried out in January 2013, was to provide a platform for citizens to more actively monitor PSM and health services, as well as to provide an evidence base for advocating policy reform in the health sector—with an an emphasis on improved access to essential medicines. Of the 20 health facilities selected in the nine counties surveyed, nine of the facilities (one in each county) targeted for the survey had participated in a social accountability (Sacc) project carried out by the Ministry of Health in partnership with the World Bank Country Office. The eleven other facilities from the same counties (one from each county except Nairobi and Homabay counties that had two) had not participated in the Sacc project.

In December 2013, the Medicines Transparency Alliance (MeTA) in Uganda carried out a study, "Client Satisfaction with Services in Uganda's Public Health Facilities," in 10 districts and 202 health facilities across the country, and more than 3,000 patients as well as nearly 500 frontline service delivery personnel and policy level staff. Survey tools were designed on the basis of theory that *when citizens are empowered, they can advocate effectively for and demand quality services and accountability at various levels of government.* The objectives were to: (i) determine the level of client satisfaction with health service delivery in public health facilities in Uganda; (ii) establish the availability of medicines in these health facilities; and (iii) determine the level of citizen empowerment in advocating better service delivery at health facilities. This was to establish a baseline in each of these three areas and to identify opportunities where collaborative interventions could accelerate reforms. The key findings reveal challenges in client satisfaction with health service delivery (especially at lower levels of care), low citizen empowerment to advocate better service delivery, and significant bottlenecks in access to laboratory supplies.

They include the following:

- The level of satisfaction with services in public health facilities was rated at 47 percent.
- Generally, the nearer patients were to the nation's capital, the higher their satisfaction with health services.
- Satisfaction increased through levels of care, with the highest at referral hospitals.

Included in a comprehensive list of recommendations for various stakeholder groups were:

- District Health Teams should better monitor stock status at facilities to trigger, facilitate and inform stock transfers between facilities or back to the National Medical Stores for wider redistribution.
- The Ministry of Health, along with its partners, should develop tools for continuous monitoring of clients' satisfaction in all health centers across the country.
- The National Medical Stores should propose and pursue necessary amendments to the rules and regulations in the Public Procurement and Disposal of Assets Act, to enable the agency to use local partner agencies for procurement.

Uganda's Commissioner of Community Health Services launched the report in February 2014 on behalf of the Minister for Primary Health Care, and pledged the government's commitment to work together with MeTA and key stakeholders to implement the report's recommendations in order to improve services.

PHASE IV

Moving ahead: MeTA's report sparked a broad multistakeholder conversation on specific roles of government, civil society, and the private sector in addressing some of the key findings emerging from the study. As a result of the study, MeTA—at the request of the Ministry of Health and other partners—has been tasked with implementing some of the recommendations in two selected districts. MeTA will:

- Meet with all relevant political and technical stakeholders at the national and district level to explain the findings of the study, and obtain critical buy-in for a pilot of recommendations.
- Strengthen the capacity of Local Government Authorities (LGAs) to better monitor health service delivery at the facility level. This will entail training members of Health Unit Management Committees as well as Village Health Teams on their roles and responsibilities vis-à-vis health service delivery monitoring. MeTA will also assist these local authorities to gain a better understanding of the Rights Based Approach to health, an underlying principle of service delivery.
- Design and implement a comprehensive community score card program in selected communities to monitor health service delivery and enhance performance in specific health facilities. This will involve identifying and training local facilitators, sensitizing local communities, and developing a score card that incorporates the necessary indicators linked to the findings of the study.

- Sensitize local communities on the use of Grievance Redress Mechanisms. The sensitization process will include a thorough review of redress and complaint-handling mechanisms to ascertain what is currently offered to the public, what works well, what does not, what is missing and what should be available. The review should highlight improvements needed and how they can be integrated into health facility operations.
- Design and implement a community-based program to allow health facilities and LGAs to better disseminate information on issues such as health facility expenditures, medicine schedules, patient charter, etc.

Cases of Mapping Outcomes: Improving Governance in Pharmaceutical Procurement and Supply Chain Management in Kenya, Tanzania and Uganda (2013)

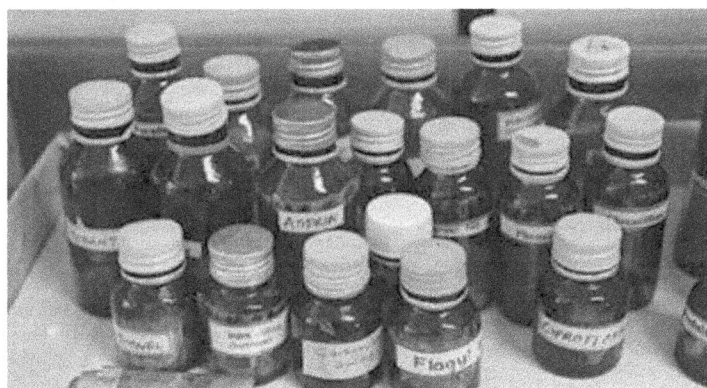

Goal
Improve citizen access to essential medicines in Kenya, Tanzania and Uganda.

Problem
Challenges in pharmaceutical procurement and supply chain management—such as poor coordination between varied actors, inefficiency and misallocation of public resources—result in waste and limit citizens' access to essential medicines at affordable prices and of good quality.

Objective
Strengthen transparency, accountability and efficiency in government pharmaceutical procurement and supply chain management to promote value for money and achieve more with less.

Since 2010, Kenya, Tanzania and Uganda have made significant progress in strengthening multi-stakeholder engagement to facilitate greater transparency, accountability and efficiency in Pharmaceutical Procurement and Supply Chain Management (PSM). The increased collaboration between state and non-state actors, which has emerged as a result of this engagement, is integral to improving access to essential medicines, the goal of WBI's Improving Governance in Pharmaceutical Procurement and Supply Chain Management Initiative.

In January–March 2013, WBI mapped the outcomes[1] of this initiative using a customized outcomeharvesting tool.[2] This visual map (figure B.1) presents the sequence of outcomes achieved by change agents—the leaders, coalitions and organizations involved in the process. The map illustrates how the outcomes connected and built on each other over time to form multi-actor, institutional processes for change to address the initiative's objectives and goal.

WBI team members identified and formulated the outcomes, presenting an explanation of their significance and how WBI had contributed—directly or indirectly, in a small or big way, intentionally or not—by catalyzing or empowering the change agents to take new actions. Then, roughly 20% of the outcomes were independently substantiated for credibility in the mapping exercise.

Background

According to the European Health Care Fraud and Corruption Network and the World Health Organization, annual global health expenditure stands at about US $5.3 trillion. Of this outlay, US $750 billion (18%) is spent in the pharmaceutical market, while consumers lose about US $300 billion more to human error and corruption. Together, total expenditure for pharmaceuticals and the cost of corruption combined exceeds US $1 trillion, or approximately 1/5th of what is spent globally on health care.

Pharmaceutical procurement is particularly prone to poor governance, since it entails complex processes that involve many stakeholders, including government ministries, procurement agencies, manufacturers, hospitals, distributors and citizens as the ultimate clients. When pharmaceutical procurement and supply chain systems work effectively, they offer high levels of quality, cost-effectiveness, product availability, transparency, accountability and value for money in the use of public funds.

The effort to improve these systems is especially critical in emerging markets, where pharmaceutical spending is 20–30% higher than the global average. International reference prices and cross-country knowledge sharing are thus critical to low-income countries obtaining fair prices on the global pharmaceutical market.

In 2010, WBI's Health Systems and Open Governance practices jointly launched the Improving Governance in Pharmaceutical Procurement and Supply Chain Management Initiative in Kenya, Tanzania, and Uganda. The initiative focuses on addressing weak governance in PSM, including legal and regulatory issues, organizational inefficiencies, challenges of information asymmetries and poor multi-stakeholder coordination and collective problem solving.[3]

The initiative seeks to create and build the capacity of multi-stakeholder coalitions comprising public and private sectors and CSOs (including academia, media and faith-based organizations) in Tanzania, Kenya and Uganda. Through capacity development, WBI provides the coalitions with cutting-edge tools to build strong relationships across stakeholder groups, understand and address the political economy of health sector reforms, enhance technical understanding of pharmaceutical PSM issues and engage demand-side actors in generating

FIGURE B.1 **Map of Outcomes Showing How Changes Were Connected and Built over a Four-Year Timeframe**

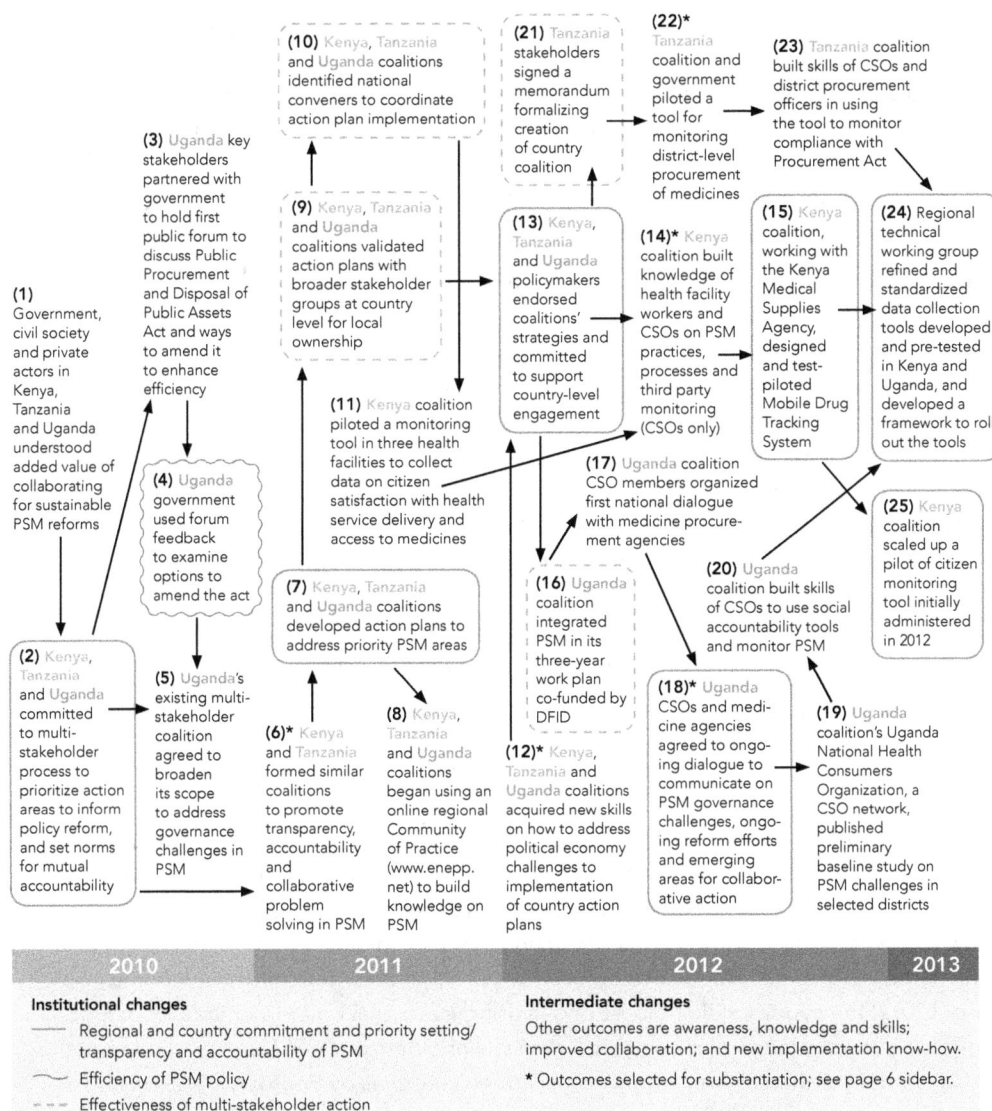

(10) Kenya, Tanzania and Uganda coalitions identified national conveners to coordinate action plan implementation

(21) Tanzania stakeholders signed a memorandum formalizing creation of country coalition

(22)* Tanzania coalition and government piloted a tool for monitoring district-level procurement of medicines

(23) Tanzania coalition built skills of CSOs and district procurement officers in using the tool to monitor compliance with Procurement Act

(3) Uganda key stakeholders partnered with government to hold first public forum to discuss Public Procurement and Disposal of Public Assets Act and ways to amend it to enhance efficiency

(9) Kenya, Tanzania and Uganda coalitions validated action plans with broader stakeholder groups at country level for local ownership

(13) Kenya, Tanzania and Uganda policymakers endorsed coalitions' strategies and committed to support country-level engagement

(14)* Kenya coalition built knowledge of health facility workers and CSOs on PSM practices, processes and third party monitoring (CSOs only)

(15) Kenya coalition, working with the Kenya Medical Supplies Agency, designed and test-piloted Mobile Drug Tracking System

(24) Regional technical working group refined and standardized data collection tools developed and pre-tested in Kenya and Uganda, and developed a framework to roll out the tools

(1) Government, civil society and private actors in Kenya, Tanzania and Uganda understood added value of collaborating for sustainable PSM reforms

(4) Uganda government used forum feedback to examine options to amend the act

(11) Kenya coalition piloted a monitoring tool in three health facilities to collect data on citizen satisfaction with health service delivery and access to medicines

(17) Uganda coalition CSO members organized first national dialogue with medicine procurement agencies

(25) Kenya coalition scaled up a pilot of citizen monitoring tool initially administered in 2012

(7) Kenya, Tanzania and Uganda coalitions developed action plans to address priority PSM areas

(16) Uganda coalition integrated PSM in its three-year work plan co-funded by DFID

(20) Uganda coalition built skills of CSOs to use social accountability tools and monitor PSM

(2) Kenya, Tanzania and Uganda committed to multi-stakeholder process to prioritize action areas to inform policy reform, and set norms for mutual accountability

(5) Uganda's existing multi-stakeholder coalition agreed to broaden its scope to address governance challenges in PSM

(6)* Kenya and Tanzania formed similar coalitions to promote transparency, accountability and collaborative problem solving in PSM

(8) Kenya, Tanzania and Uganda coalitions began using an online regional Community of Practice (www.enepp. net) to build knowledge on PSM

(12)* Kenya, Tanzania and Uganda coalitions acquired new skills on how to address political economy challenges to implementation of country action plans

(18)* Uganda CSOs and medicine agencies agreed to ongoing dialogue to communicate on PSM governance challenges, ongoing reform efforts and emerging areas for collaborative action

(19) Uganda coalition's Uganda National Health Consumers Organization, a CSO network, published preliminary baseline study on PSM challenges in selected districts

| 2010 | 2011 | 2012 | 2013 |

Institutional changes

—— Regional and country commitment and priority setting/ transparency and accountability of PSM

〜 Efficiency of PSM policy

- - - Effectiveness of multi-stakeholder action

Intermediate changes

Other outcomes are awareness, knowledge and skills; improved collaboration; and new implementation know-how.

* Outcomes selected for substantiation; see page 6 sidebar.

evidence-based data to inform policymaking. These capacity development components are intended to strengthen collaborative action toward reforms, which is expected to accelerate PSM change processes and ultimately improve access to medicines.

Tanzania, Kenya, and Uganda have initiated country-level processes that have the potential to reform pharmaceutical PSM processes. They possess both technical and leadership capacity enhanced through structured learning, knowledge exchange and peer-to=peer learning that facilitate regional multi-stakeholderled efforts to improve governance in PSM.

Accelerating Health Reforms through Collective Action • http://dx.doi.org/10.1596/978-1-4648-0287-4

Outcome Areas

The process of change from this initiative can be seen in three streams of outcomes that represent the major change paths (figure B.2). All of the outcomes were analyzed and classified according to the types of change they achieved. They were then grouped based on how they connected to each other to form a story for change. Outcomes that correspond to those in figure B.1 are indicated with bracketed numbers below.

OUTCOME AREA 1: REGIONAL COMMITMENT TO IMPROVE ACCESS TO MEDICINES

In this initiative, regional and country-level commitment helped drive effective and sustained actions.

In June 2010, pharmaceutical procurement agencies, public procurement oversight authorities, ministries of health, civil society actors and private companies in Kenya, Tanzania and Uganda acknowledged governance weaknesses in PSM and came together regionally to discuss approaches for achieving more sustainable reforms. These actors recognized the limitations of working through the customary approach of "silos," with little collaboration across stakeholder groups. Stakeholders realized the value presented through synergistic approaches to problem solving, and, therefore, committed to pursuing a more systematic, collaborative approach to influence reforms. [1, 2]

More important, stakeholders viewed working together as a critical strategy toward making inroads at a time when health policy reform was a national priority in all three countries. The collaborative address of systemic challenges in PSM promised to leverage stakeholder strengths and expertise; create a level playing field for constructive dialogue between multiple stakeholders; facilitate consensus building about reform priorities; and establish mutual accountability for results.

WBI held extensive consultations at the country level to elicit stakeholder feedback on a proposed concept note for a multi-stakeholder approach for strengthening good governance in pharmaceutical PSM. Through facilitated discussions, WBI helped stakeholders understand the link between the slow progress on PSM and working in silos and demonstrated the potential for state and non-state actors to work collaboratively for stronger and more effective reforms.

In April 2011, the country stakeholders began using a regional online Community of Practice (CoP) to build knowledge and commitment of stakeholders on PSM (see www.enepp.net). [8] The CoP had more than 350 members from all three countries by February 2013. Having a CoP became important for advancing regional knowledge exchange between practitioners in all three countries, and providing a "safe" space to share challenges, innovative solutions and resources to help move forward sensitive reforms.

WBI designed, developed and launched the online platform during a regional workshop in Kenya, held April 2011. WBI facilitated membership of participants at the workshop and other stakeholders at the country level from the public, private and civil society sectors and development partners.

In April 2012, representatives of multi-stakeholder coalitions in each country gathered regionally to discuss their respective challenges, explore approaches for addressing the political economy of reforms, reprioritize their action plans and set realistic timelines. [12] This refinement of country action plans was necessary since the multi-stakeholder coalitions were

FIGURE B.2 **Change Strategy Showing How Change Happened to Advance Progress Toward Goal**

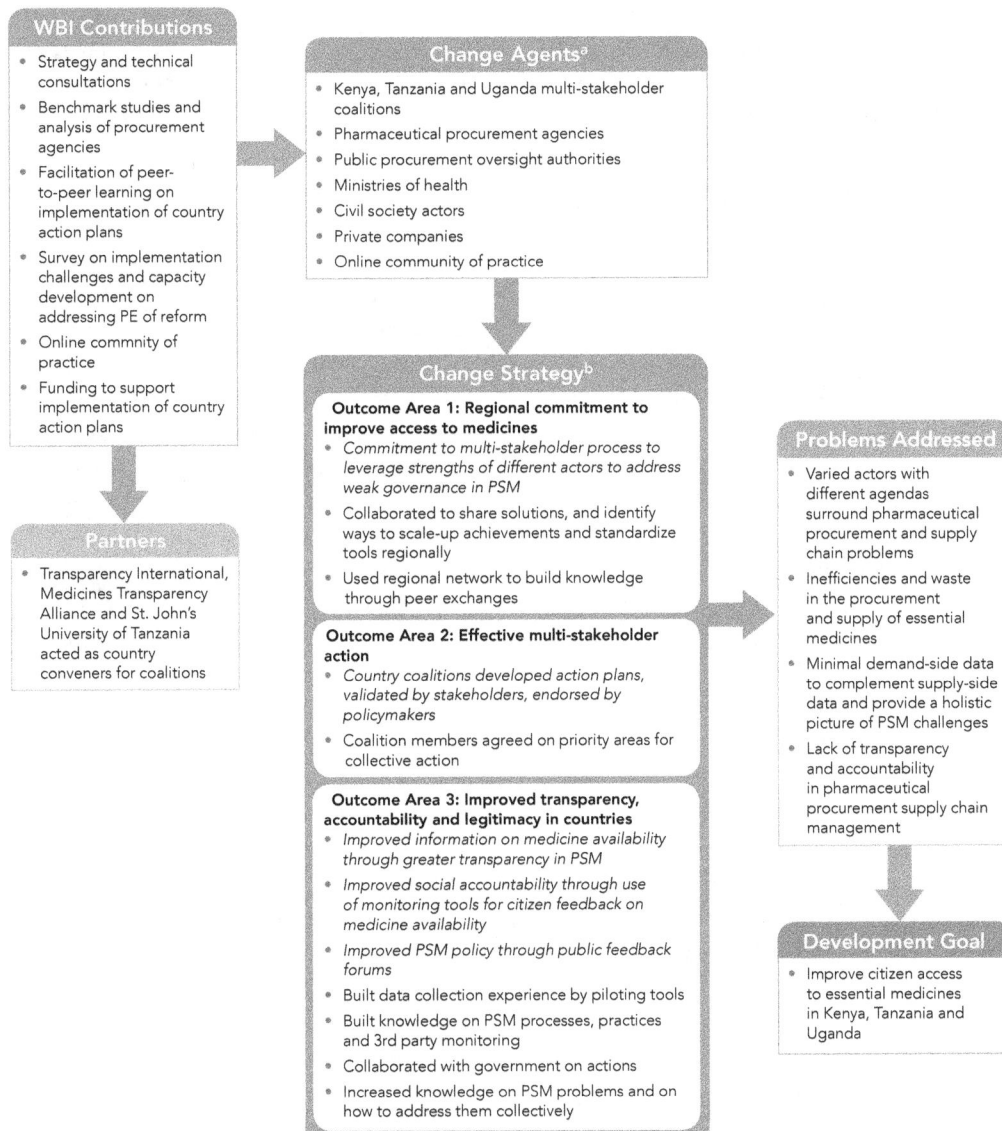

WBI Contributions

- Strategy and technical consultations
- Benchmark studies and analysis of procurement agencies
- Facilitation of peer-to-peer learning on implementation of country action plans
- Survey on implementation challenges and capacity development on addressing PE of reform
- Online commnity of practice
- Funding to support implementation of country action plans

Change Agents[a]

- Kenya, Tanzania and Uganda multi-stakeholder coalitions
- Pharmaceutical procurement agencies
- Public procurement oversight authorities
- Ministries of health
- Civil society actors
- Private companies
- Online community of practice

Partners

- Transparency International, Medicines Transparency Alliance and St. John's University of Tanzania acted as country conveners for coalitions

Change Strategy[b]

Outcome Area 1: Regional commitment to improve access to medicines
- *Commitment to multi-stakeholder process to leverage strengths of different actors to address weak governance in PSM*
- Collaborated to share solutions, and identify ways to scale-up achievements and standardize tools regionally
- Used regional network to build knowledge through peer exchanges

Outcome Area 2: Effective multi-stakeholder action
- *Country coalitions developed action plans, validated by stakeholders, endorsed by policymakers*
- Coalition members agreed on priority areas for collective action

Outcome Area 3: Improved transparency, accountability and legitimacy in countries
- *Improved information on medicine availability through greater transparency in PSM*
- *Improved social accountability through use of monitoring tools for citizen feedback on medicine availability*
- *Improved PSM policy through public feedback forums*
- Built data collection experience by piloting tools
- Built knowledge on PSM processes, practices and 3rd party monitoring
- Collaborated with government on actions
- Increased knowledge on PSM problems and on how to address them collectively

Problems Addressed

- Varied actors with different agendas surround pharmaceutical procurement and supply chain problems
- Inefficiencies and waste in the procurement and supply of essential medicines
- Minimal demand-side data to complement supply-side data and provide a holistic picture of PSM challenges
- Lack of transparency and accountability in pharmaceutical procurement supply chain management

Development Goal

- Improve citizen access to essential medicines in Kenya, Tanzania and Uganda

[a]Change agents are leaders, groups or organizations from government or non-state that drive change.

[b]Change strategy is how change happened to advance progress toward the goal and objectives—the development problems addressed, types of outcomes achieved, WBI contributions and partners involved. A change strategy may include different types of change processes or streams depending on the complexity of the multi-actor institutional changes involved in a program.

experiencing implementation challenges and needed to review their priorities to identify areas where they could have the most impact. A key concern across the coalitions was how to address perceived mistrust between actors, as well as promote a more equitable balance of power among stakeholders to ease coordination, forge collaboration and facilitate attainment of shared objectives. The country coalitions also prioritized the role of demand side actors in generating an evidence base on health service delivery and access to medicines at the facility level to better inform policy dialogue.

WBI administered a survey to members of the multi-stakeholder coalitions in Kenya, Tanzania and Uganda in late 2011 to understand the implementation challenges the coalitions faced and identify areas where WBI could provide capacity development and technical assistance. WBI's Greater than Leadership Program designed a five-day workshop for the coalitions on "Strengthening Multi-stakeholder Coalitions Through Leadership Action." WBI also provided funding to accelerate implementation of the refined action plans.

In October 2012, a regional team of experts representing government and civil society from Kenya, Tanzania and Uganda refined, standardized and finalized data collection tools developed and pretested by the coalitions. The technical working group of experts also developed a monitoring and evaluation framework to guide the refinement, finalization and roll out of the tools. [24] They identified the need for two supplementary data collection tools: a Citizen Empowerment Tool to determine the existence of and assess the efficacy of Grievance Redress Mechanisms in receiving and responding to citizen feedback on health service delivery, as well as a Stock Monitoring Tool to track stock levels of tracer medicines in selected health facilities in all three countries. The set of harmonized tools will aid cross-country comparison and analyses to gain a broader picture of citizen satisfaction with health services, access to medicines and citizen empowerment across the region.

WBI facilitated the technical working group meeting to refine, standardize and finalize the data collection tools, as well as develop supplementary tools and outline an appropriate M&E framework.

So, over 30 months multi-stakeholder processes had leveraged the strengths of different actors to address weak governance in PSM. These commitments materialized through: improved regional recognition of the value of state and non-state actors engaging collaboratively on PSM; enhanced regional networking to build knowledge, shared solutions and identified ways to scale-up achievements; and development and review of new and innovative data collection tools to generate demand-side evidence to complement national data on health service delivery and access to medicines.

OUTCOME AREA 2: EFFECTIVE MULTI-STAKEHOLDER ACTION

Multi-stakeholder coalitions became important to address PSM in the country context. In 2011, an existing multi-stakeholder group in Uganda—Medicines Transparency Alliance (MeTA)—agreed to broaden its scope to become the country coalition to address governance challenges in PSM. [5] Rather than establish a new multi-stakeholder coalition, it was important to leverage existing capacity by joining forces with MeTA, which has been in Uganda since 2007 and has established networks with both state and non-state actors. Consequently, MeTA integrated PSM in its three-year plan co-funded by the United Kingdom Department for International Development (DFID). [16] This secured funding for the broadened mandate of MeTA to address PSM and gave it more credibility to do so. It was a quick win for the coalition by building on its existing networks.

SUBSTANTIATION OF OUTCOMES

To verify the accuracy of the outcomes mapped and enrich WBI's understanding of them, the external consultant selected 5 outcomes [6, 12, 14, 18, 22] and asked 15 people independent of WBI but knowledgeable about the change to review each and record whether they agree with the outcome as described. Thirteen people responded and all "fully agreed" with the description as formulated of the outcome and its significance. Excerpts of the substantiators' comments on the outcomes achieved:

"The commitment of the high-level policy makers was important to the work of the PSM coalition as it will enable their work get the recognition and support it needs in high-level decisionmaking that affects the PSM. The bringing together of the PSM Coalitions and high-level policy makers needed a champion and WBI played that role well and in a timely manner."

—Ramadhan Mlinga, Chief Executive Officer, Public Procurement Regulatory Authority, Tanzania

"While such multi-stakeholder coalitions are important, they need to be better aligned with overall World Bank engagement in the country level and contribute to better policy dialogue on improving participation of stakeholders and enhanced transparency. Therefore, I would like to see much stronger emphasis on linkage with the Bank's long-term engagement in the outcome. This way, WBI contributions will provide more sustainable gains."

— Gandham N.V. Ramana, Lead Health Specialist, World Bank

"To improve lives of the citizens can only be successful with support of the government (high-level policy makers), failure to which interventions increasingly achieve minimal results. Working with government senior officials has enabled the civil society to fill in gaps within the policy system, a key gap being monitoring of impact of the government expended resources. Then direct feedback to high-level policy makers. The Kenya Medical Supply Agency has been a key beneficiary of this type of CSO monitoring of their services."

— Debra Gichio, Program Officer, Transparency International, Kenya

"This meeting [National Medicines Dialogue in May 2012] brought a number of agencies and CSOs together. Most especially the district CSOs were able to meet the executive directors of the National Drug Authority, Joint Medical Stores, National Medical Stores and Ministry Of Health. In fact one of the participants said 'now this is a dream come true because I have always wanted to see National Medical Stores.'"

—Robinah Kaitiritimba, Executive Director, Uganda National Health Consumers Organisation

At the same time, various actors from Kenya and Tanzania formed similar multi-stakeholder coalitions to promote greater transparency, accountability and collaborative problem solving in PSM. [6] In Kenya, the Forum for Transparency and Accountability in Pharmaceutical Procurement (FoTAPP) was established in May 2011. The group comprises public sector agencies, including the Ministry of Health, Kenya Medical Supplies Agency, Public Procurement and Oversight Authority, Kenya Anti-corruption Commission and the Pharmacy and Poisons Board; civil society; donor partners; the private sector; and academia.

In Tanzania, 22 organizations, including the Public Procurement Regulatory Authority, Ministry of Health and Social Services, Food and Drugs Authority, and Medical Stores Department, as well as 13 CSOs, signed a Memorandum of Understanding to formally launch the coalition. [21] The coalition has since expanded its members. Formalization of the coalition was important in the country context to create a legitimate entity recognized by government, private sector and civil society as the vehicle for promoting transparency, accountability and efficiency in PSM. Each country coalition developed action plans to, for the first time, tackle country-specific PSM challenges through a multi-stakeholder approach. [7] The key was building a shared understanding of priorities and responsibilities among the different stakeholders. In view of resource constraints and competing priorities, the coalitions tried to identify areas where they could achieve quick and high-impact outcomes.

WBI facilitated and convened a regional workshop in Kenya in April 2011 and attended by coalition representatives. At the event, WBI provided tools and resources to guide stakeholders in establishing country coalitions, developing country action plans and identifying common areas of interest where all three countries could engage and share their experiences though the regional CoP. WBI also provided input on Memoranda of Understanding.

Beyond establishing the core membership of the country coalitions, each country group held broader national consultations to seek broad-based buy-in for the country action plans developed and to ensure local ownership for priority areas of collaborative engagement. [9] With this endorsement at the national level, the coalitions identified country conveners responsible for coordinating multi-stakeholder activities. [10] This effort established a focal point or secretariat for the coalitions' day-to-day functioning, including organizing meetings and following up on decisions.

WBI provided guidance to the country consultation processes led by the coalitions, and contacted World Bank staff in the country to facilitate relationships with key government stakeholders. By April 2012, high-level policymakers from Kenya, Tanzania and Uganda had endorsed the country action plans and committed themselves to supporting activities of the country coalitions [13]. Up until this moment, the government representatives in the coalitions had limited authority to commit to specific interventions, which often relied on the buy-in and political willingness of higher-level officials, such as heads of agencies, within the public sector. This formal endorsement from policy makers:

- Demonstrated political support for the coalition's PSM strategies
- Linked coalition activities to relevant country reforms
- Helped establish supporting relationships between policymakers and the coalitions necessary for strengthening partnership with the government
- Helped lay the groundwork for joint demand- and supply-side data collection and other activities that the coalitions prioritized in their strategies

WBI convened a high-level policy dialogue among the country policymakers in Uganda, Kenya and Tanzania in April 2012 after recognizing the difficulties that the country coalitions faced in gaining traction on their activities and priorities. WBI facilitated knowledge exchange between the country conveners in Uganda, Kenya and Tanzania, and guided the sharing of experiences on how to formalize the multi-stakeholder coalitions in-country.

In sum, building on regional commitment, multistakeholder country coalitions mobilized in Uganda, Kenya and Tanzania to take action to achieve improved practices in PSM.

OUTCOME AREA 3: IMPROVED TRANSPARENCY, ACCOUNTABILITY AND EFFICIENCY

Since 2010, the coalitions have contributed to improving open dialogue around governance vulnerabilities in pharmaceutical PSM, and in working together to pilot innovative solutions to ensuring greater transparency, accountability and efficiency in PSM. Key country-specific achievements include:

Uganda Coalition—Medicines Transparency Alliance (MeTA)

In July 2010, MeTA, in partnership with the Public Procurement and Disposal of Public Assets Authority (PPDPA), held the first public forum to discuss the 2003 Public Procurement and Disposal of Public Assets Act and opportunities to amend it to enhance efficiency in procure-ment of essential medicines, among other things. [3] This action tested the multi-stakeholder approach in engaging non-state actors in providing input into ongoing legislative reform. This led the PPDPA to review the act that governed its activities, examining options for amend-ments. [4] The success demonstrated the power of multi-stakeholder collaboration and signalled a shift in the way the PPDPA traditionally engaged, which previously involved minimal engagement with non-state actors.

In May 2012, MeTA—under the leadership of Uganda National Health Consumers Organisation (UNHCO)—organized the first national dialogue on medicines. [17] This meeting brought together key agencies, particularly the National Medical Stores, the National Drug Authority, the Drug Moni-toring Unit, and the Joint Medical Stores of the Ministry of Health and pharmaceutical councils. The CSOs and medicines agencies agreed to an ongoing dialogue to openly collaborate and com-municate on PSM governance challenges. [18] This dialogue helped establish trust between the agencies and coalition and created legitimacy for the coalition to address PSM challenges.

In June 2012, UNHCO also published a preliminary baseline study—based on research from four districts in Uganda—that helped identify key gaps in PSM and highlighted interven-tions where the coalition could leverage its comparative advantages. [19] The study helped to provide up-to-date information on PSM challenges and further grounded the proposed interventions and priorities of the coalition within the country context.

Also in June 2012, MeTA trained CSOs on social accountability tools and their role in moni-toring PSM at the health facility level. [20] This training started to build the capacity of CSOs to monitor PSM, as well as to raise awareness about effective and transparent PSM processes.

WBI contributed funding for the coalition to organize cand implement national dialogue activities and helped create a platform for open discussion between the medicine agencies. At the request of PPDPA, WBI provided examples of similar acts in Africa to help them think through amendments for Uganda. WBI leveraged resources from UNHCO to engage technical experts to develop the baseline study to inform the coalition's priorities. WBI organized a Regional Training of Trainers' Workshop on PSM attended by Uganda coalition members.

Kenya Coalition—Forum for Transparency and Accountability in Pharmaceutical Procurement (FoTAPP)

In June 2012, FoTAPP developed and test-piloted a Citizen Monitoring Tool in three health facilities in Nairobi County to collect data on citizens' level of satisfaction with health services and their access to medicines—in terms of physical availability as well as affordability. [11] The tool enabled citizens to provide feedback on their level of satisfaction with health services. The success of the exercise also indicated the potential for demand-side data collection to generate evidence to inform policy dialogue. The coalition also built knowledge of health facility workers and CSOs on PSM practices and CSO monitoring. [14] This training built the understanding of both supply- and demand-side actors on their roles to improve outcomes in access to medicines. Such understanding is required both for the effective use of monitoring tools and for building consensus on reform possibilities.

Additionally, FoTAPP, working closely with the Kenya Medical Supplies Agency (KEMSA), designed and test-piloted a Mobile Drug Tracking System (MDTS). The MDTS provides citizens, community health workers, health facilities and health management committees with real-time information on medicine availability in selected health facilities. For patients with specific diseases—tuberculosis, HIV/AIDS, diabetes—this system is especially useful to track the availability of medicines in health facilities, making it more efficient to obtain life-saving drugs and reduce transaction costs. [15] It allows the tracking of medical commodities from KEMSA warehouses to health facilities, making it easier for the demand-side to monitor delivery of essential medicines. The development of this tool also represents a practical example of collaboration with government on the delivery of demand-side tools.

In February 2013, FoTAPP completed a pilot of a more extensive data collection exercise in 20 health facilities in nine counties across the country. This scaled up the pilot of the Citizen Monitoring Tool initially administered in 2012. [25] The roll out of the data collection exercise will provide a baseline to help measure the impact of the coalitions' interventions over the next five years and determine efficacy of the multi-stakeholder approach in facilitating PSM reforms and improving access to medicines.

WBI provided the Kenya coalition funding to support the development of the Citizen Monitoring Tool for data collection, the capacity building workshop, and in collaboration with KEMSA, to engage an ICT consultant to design software for the MDTS. WBI provided technical support to the team in developing a proposal for funding through the Social Development Civil Society Fund, which selected the coalition as a recipient of US $100,000 to support scale up of the Citizen Monitoring Tool pilot.

Tanzania Coalition

In June 2012, the Tanzania coalition, in partnership with the Public Procurement Regulatory Authority, developed a procurement monitoring tool to examine the processes used to procure pharmaceuticals at the district level and to determine their compliance with the Public Procurement Act. [22] They, along with the Muhimbili University of Health and Allied Sciences and St. John's University of Tanzania, also trained CSOs, district procurement officers from

Dodoma region and representatives of the Medical Stores Department and test-piloted the tool in six districts in the Dodoma region. [23]

Given the substantial resources allocated to pharmaceutical procurement at the district level, the coalition prioritized procurement monitoring to ensure resources were being used efficiently and in compliance with Public Procurement Act. Such monitoring would help advocate value for money in PSM and contribute to improved access to medicines. The coalition is working closely with the regulatory authority to prioritize reform areas based on recommendations from the final procurement monitoring report.

WBI reviewed the draft procurement monitoring tool and provided substantive comments for enhancement.

In sum, the multi-stakeholder country coalitions in Uganda, Kenya and Tanzania are increasingly taking actions to improve transparency, accountability and efficiency in PSM through inclusive dialogue to influence policy; generation of baseline data that help prioritize reform areas for collaborative action; capacity development for key actors, especially CSOs; and innovative tools to monitor PSM at the facility level. Also important is the involvement of both supply- and demand-side actors to strengthen their respective roles in the country context to improve access to medicines.

Conclusion

Improving transparency, accountability and efficiency in PSM was pursued through collaboration between government and civil society actors, regionally and through country coalitions. Traditionally, the two stakeholder groups have not worked together to address challenges in PSM; rather, they worked in silos, with minimal communication and cooperation. Through the development of joint country action plans, the multi-stakeholder coalitions achieved milestones in improving partnership, specifically around the design and implementation of both demand- and supply-side tools to monitor PSM.

In **Uganda,** the successful launch and public dialogue around findings of a preliminary baseline study on PSM challenges—organized by MeTA—created a platform for continued engagement with National Medical Stores, Joint Medical Stores and the Ministry of Health. All three partners are now collaborating with the coalition to design and pilot four data collection tools in 10 districts across Uganda.

In **Kenya,** the coalition partnered for the first time with KEMSA to pilot an innovative MDTS, which allows citizens and health workers to access real-time information on medicine availability in selected health facilities.

In **Tanzania,** the coalition—in collaboration with the Public Procurement and Regulatory Authority—designed and piloted a procurement monitoring tool for use by district officers to assess the level of compliance with the Public Procurement Act.

Another area of progress has been capacity development of coalitions, particularly of civil society, to better understand, monitor and advance advocacy around PSM reforms, with an emphasis on greater transparency, accountability and efficiency.

Many of the CSOs trained through this initiate are leading data collection exercises on health service delivery in their respective communities. The initiative has also published a Training of Trainers Manual as a guide for civil society actors interested in implementing social accountability mechanisms to improve service delivery, with a focus on access to medicines.

Next Steps

Because of the change processes, the coalitions are empowered to advance outcomes of their own. There is local ownership of the process, and key relationships—especially with government—have been formed that should provide a foundation and impetus for advancing outcomes.

Nonetheless, a key challenge that remains is to ensure the full participation of the private for-profit sector to facilitate broader stakeholder engagement, support longer-term sustainability as well as sustain the momentum for reform.

Further, the importance of grounding coalition priorities in local contexts has become clear. The coalition-building experience in three countries shows how country dynamics often influence the ability and agility of the coalition. Kenya succeeded in moving quickly with its country action plans because it has a more favorable enabling environment—including a relatively mature democracy, sophisticated technology and close relationship with a government client eager to integrate citizen and demand-side feedback. It is important to understand the local dynamics in each country context and work within that framework to identify local champions that have the capacity to move reforms quickly and bring the coalition along.

Now, a key strategy for the initiative is to share the experience and early results of implementing the coalition-building approach to improving governance of PSM in East Africa. Lessons learned will provide practical guidance on the "how to" of coalition building in health service delivery and provide recommendations on applications in other country contexts. For example, the capacity developed within the coalitions can be applied to monitoring health service delivery in general, which is an area of increased demand.

In addition to continuing to contribute to outcomes in the three streams described, new outcomes are expected, particularly around implementation of joint interventions to address emerging issues that will be highlighted in the data collection exercise from all three countries.

Notes

[1] Outcomes refer to significant changes in the behavior, relationships, actions, policies or practices of a change agent that WBI has influenced, directly or indirectly, partially or wholly, intended or not. Outcomes are identified at two levels in relation to the goal: *institutional changes* relate to improvements in ownership, policy and/or organizations; and *intermediate changes* relate to improvements in awareness, knowledge and skills, collaborative processes and implementation experience. These levels are based on WBI's Capacity Development Results Framework, which provides a flexible guide for the assessment, design, and monitoring and evaluation of multi-stakeholder development efforts and associated processes of change management.

[2] Outcome mapping gathers information on outcomes across the change strategy of a program to learn from what changed, for whom, when and where, the significance of the change and how WBI contributed.

[3] While the Improving Governance in Pharmaceutical Procurement and Supply Chain Management Initiative was established in 2010, over the years it has become part of the global

movement on "Open Contracting," a multi-sector effort that seeks to promote greater transparency and accountability in the award and implementation of public sector contracts.

[4]The numbers in brackets correspond to the outcomes in figure B.1. The text that usually follows each outcome refers to its significance. The process of change the outcomes represent can be seen in figure B.2.

FOR MORE INFORMATION

Project Contacts
Yvonne Nkrumah, Senior Operations Officer, WBI Health Systems practice, ynkrumah@worldbank.org

Julia Mensah, Extended Term Consultant, WBI Health Systems practice, jmensah1@worldbank.org

Email
WBI Capacity Development and Results team at capacity4change@worldbank.org

Website
www.worldbank.org/capacity

© Copyright 2013 World Bank
WBI's Capacity Development and Results team led the outcome mapping; Jenny Gold coordinated the exercise with support from Ricardo Wilson-Grau. Sharon Fisher provided editorial and design services. Samuel Otoo provided overall guidance.

ACKNOWLEDGMENTS

Thanks to Marylou Bradley and Jilliane T Cabansag, and team members involved in the project and mapping exercise.

Thanks to:
> Dr. Gandham N.V. Ramana, Lead Health Specialist, World Bank
> Jackie Idusso, Key Account Manager, International Business Africa, Merck Sharpe and Dohme
> Dr. Eva Ombaka, Director Consultant Business Network International Tanzania Pwani
> Dr. Ramadhan Mlinga, Chief Executive Officer, Public Procurement Regulatory Authority, Tanzania
> Wachuka W. Ikua, Senior Operations Officer, World Bank
> Dr. John Munyu, Chief Executive Officer, Kenya Medical Supplies Agency
> Debra Gichio, Program Officer, Transparency International, Kenya
> Robinah Kaitiritimba, Executive Director, Uganda National Health Consumers Organisation
> Moses Kamabare, General Manager/CEO of National Medical Stores
> Apollo Muhairwe, Operations Officer, World Bank
> Dr. Laurent Shirima, Director of Capacity. Building and. Advisory Services, Tanzania
> Emmanuel Malangalila, Consultant, World Bank
> Joseph Mhando, Dean and Senior Lecturer, School of Pharmacy, St. John's University of Dar es Salaam

Pharmaceutical Procurement in Kenya, Tanzania, and Uganda: Key Findings, Best Practices, and Opportunities for Improvement (2010)

World Bank Institute

PHARMACEUTICAL PROCUREMENT IN KENYA: KEY FINDINGS, BEST PRACTICES, AND OPPORTUNITIES FOR IMPROVEMENT

Kenya at a Glance

The Kenyan Government has made sweeping progress in improving the access to and quality of country-wide pharmaceutical services. As a result of legal reform and other policy measures, the regulation of the pharmaceutical industry has been greatly enhanced. While there has been much progress, Kenya continues to confront significant obstacles in monitoring counterfeit pharmaceutical products entering the country, especially essential medicines. Finally, Kenya must continue building on the accomplishments it has made in the way of legal reform, as several of its laws remain redundant or inconsistent with international practice.

Best Practices to Share

- The well-established institutions and regulations that guide KEMSA to manage pharmaceuticals and health products efficiently are of note. Additionally, KEMSA has partnered with the Kenya Anti Corruption Commission to advance accountability and transparency within the institution, and between institutions and suppliers.

- Kenya is home to a vibrant array of civil society organizations engaged in improving access to medicines nationwide. This includes organizations such as HAI Africa, a group which supports improved health outcomes through access to pharmaceuticals as part of their mission to promote safe access to essential medicines in Kenya.

- Kenya has recently made strides to reform the legal framework regulating pharmaceutical procurement, efforts which include the revision of Chapter 244 of the Pharmacy and Poisons Act, the establishment of The Public Procurement Oversight Authority, the reorganization of the Kenya Medical Supplies Agency, and the reworking of both the Kenya Essential Medicines List (KEML) and the Standard Treatment Guidelines (STG) in June 2010.

- The installation of an ERP system indicates progress towards transparency and accountability, as well as the minimization of manual operations and margins of error within each step of procurement.

Opportunities for Improvement

Kenya's pharmaceutical procurement processes could benefit from:

- Implementing and adhering to acquisition protocol

- Enhancing coordination between various institutions involved in pharmaceutical procurement

- Improving transparency of information to ensure efficiency and compliance to regulation; specifically, making the post-bid opening stage of procurement information formally and officially accessible

- Allowing KEMSA independence with respect to budget expenditure

- Continuing the process of legal reform, as several laws continue to be outmoded or contradictory to standard international practice

- Combating delays in pharmaceutical delivery, product stock outs, and insufficient quantities of essential medicines

Priority Areas for Action

Kenyan stakeholders agreed to focus on the following areas in their efforts to continue improving procurement practice in Kenya:

- Strengthen information management systems (between regulator and procurement agency)

- Review all legislation that affects procurement entities

- Make KEMSA more autonomous with respect to budget expenditure

- Emphasize capacity-building for civil society organizations to improve their watchdog function

- Participate in the WBI (regional) network of procurement practitioners to foster peer-to-peer learning

- Strengthen the legal framework to enable wider participation in the procurement process

- Invest in capacity-building measures for E-procurement to promote transparency

- Reduce the number of vertical, parallel systems and integrate these systems

- Deepen collaboration among multi-stakeholders at the national level

World Bank Institute

PHARMACEUTICAL PROCUREMENT IN TANZANIA: KEY FINDINGS, BEST PRACTICES, AND OPPORTUNITIES FOR IMPROVEMENT

Tanzania at a Glance

The Tanzanian government has made the health sector a priority over the past decade, which has led to the adoption of several best practices within the realm of pharmaceutical procurement and an overall improvement in various key health indicators in the country. Namely, operations at Tanzania's Medical Stores Department have greatly improved in recent years, and the country has made progress in addressing procurement-related governance issues through the Public Procurement Act of 2004. Challenges Tanzania must address moving forward will be to further strengthen the regulatory framework guiding procurement, improve coordination efforts between actors involved in procurement, and increase accountability mechanisms regulating the system.

Best Practices to Share

- Tanzania's Public Procurement Act of 2004, which is a successful working model for decentralized public sector procurement, is sustained by a strong Public Procurement Regulatory Authority (PPRA) that has carried out very effective training for procurement entities.

- The PPRA offers a solid example of effective regulation for public sector procurement; specifically, the PPRA's capacity-building programs for PEs have had a strong positive impact, while the procedural forms have served as a practical guide to the tender process and in maintaining accurate records of procedural transactions.

- Tanzania's Medical Stores Department (MSD) Procurement Management Unit (PMU) exemplifies a number of best practices, including the contract management flow chart, which acts as a useful guide to contract management, and the vendor rating tool, which provides an unbiased way of recording and rating vendor performance to ensure that inefficient and unreliable contractors are identified and avoided in future transactions.

- Finally, the MSD's planned use of the Enterprise Resource Program (ERP) will be a groundbreaking initiative from which other procurement professionals can learn.

Opportunities for Improvement

Several areas require additional attention, including:

- Inadequate coordination in procurement planning

- Necessary improvements to the legal and regulatory structures surrounding procurement

- The need for stronger accountability mechanisms

- The need for increased communication between stakeholders

- Capacity limitations at the national and decentralized levels.

- The weak involvement of civil society

- A surfeit of tools and methods tracking procurement

Priority Areas for Action

Stakeholders in Tanzania agreed to take steps to improve the following:

- National-level quantification and procurement planning

- Facility-level quantification

- The role of CSOs in the interaction between providers and end-users

- Human Resources development and deployment

- Multi-stakeholder relations, especially public/private partnerships

- Regional collaboration and sharing of information

- Private sector supplier assessment

- General risk assessment methodologies

World Bank Institute

Pharmaceutical Procurement in Uganda: Key Findings, Best Practices, and Opportunities for Improvement

Uganda at a Glance

The Ugandan Government has established several effective national systems regulating pharmaceutical procurement processes. Due to reform and development efforts over the past decade, Uganda now has solid legal and regulatory frameworks governing procurement. Moving forward, Uganda must face several challenges in the effort to build upon this recent progress; the most major challenges the country has yet to face include implementing existing policies and regulations and improving coordination efforts to increase the efficiency of the system.

Best Practices to Share

- The multi-stakeholder collaboration facilitated through MeTA Uganda (Medicines Transparency Alliance) successfully promoted discourse and cross-sectoral knowledge-sharing. MeTA Uganda effectively engaged the private sector and Civil Society in reviewing the National Pharmaceutical Sector Strategic Plan, promoted the disclosure of information on volumes and values of medicines imported into Uganda by the NDA, and pursued the amendment of the procurement Act and Anti-Counterfeit Goods Bill. MeTA has also paved the way for the private sector to access information on the procurement of pharmaceuticals.

- The participation of civil society organizations such as The Coalition for Health Promotion and Social Development (HEPS), which promotes increased access to affordable essential medicines, is another laudable practice within Uganda.

- The establishment of several key pieces of legislation passed in the last decade, including the National Medicines Policy and the Public Procurement and Disposal of Public Assets Act, is also a noteworthy practice.

- Other best practices include the release of information regarding the results of bidding processes on the part of NMS, and Uganda's efforts to collaborate with other regional partners.

Opportunities for Improvement

Several areas require additional attention, including:

- The overly-bureaucratic public sector procurement system

- And the need to operationalize procurement law

There remain several process gaps regarding:

- The transparency of contract and supply chain management

- The cumbersome nature of the appeals process

- The procedures and regulations surrounding accountability mechanisms and audits

- The need for inter-departmental coordination between governmental agencies regulating procurement

- And the process by which information on procurement is disclosed to the public

Priority Areas for Action

- Stakeholders agreed that Uganda could benefit from action regarding anti-corruption measures and efforts to improve transparency.

- Stakeholders discussed taking steps to improve institutional arrangements and coordination. Participants agreed that more is required to enhance and improve communication amongst stakeholders and between donors.

- Participants noted that there is the need for capacity-building among key stakeholders, particularly to encourage civil society strengthening, participation during technical evaluations of procurement, and so that informed groups could encourage transparency and accountability.

- Stakeholders agreed that the country could benefit from information generation and disclosure at multiple levels.

Code of Conduct for the Multistakeholder Group on Pharmaceutical Procurement in Tanzania

PREAMBLE

The Multistakeholder Group on Pharmaceutical Procurement in Tanzania (MSG-Pharma) is a coalition of organizations and individuals with common interest in achieving good governance in pharmaceutical procurement in Tanzania. This code of conduct is written in accordance with the provisions of the Memorandum of Understanding of the group as signed by all parties concerned. The code seeks to harness the potential of the coalition and individual members in realizing the objectives set forth in the Memorandum of Understanding, direct the management of the coalition and guide interaction between individual members.

POWERS AND CAPABILITIES OF THE COALITION

1. To define very clearly goals and objectives of the coalition and provide the final interpretation of the terms of the Memorandum of Understanding
2. To design and institute written and transparent HR, financial and office management procedures
3. To request one of the members to host the secretariat
4. To design and install good office management procedures
5. To endeavor to meet all costs of running the coalition
6. To discuss and solicit internal and external donors to fund individual activities
7. To discuss and solicit internal and external donors to provide technical expertise and assistance where required
8. To use local consultancy and technical services where available
9. To undertake data collection as will be necessary in the fulfillment of the coalition's objectives
10. To undertake procurement contract monitoring activities
11. To encourage members to register and use Enepp[1]
12. To organize meetings, workshops and seminars for members and other target groups
13. To join any group that shares common aspirations with the MSG and, consequently, present periodic reports as will be required under the terms of association of the larger group
14. To encourage and support establishment of sub-groups for the purpose of providing specialized attention to a particular issue
15. To encourage and support establishment of regional and district MSGs

16. To promote public awareness of the MSG and its activities
17. To lobby for recognition by the government and participation of government departments in the MSG
18. To lobby for recognition by development partners and their participation in the MSG
19. To establish a public relations unit to handle public communication
20. To establish a unit to coordinate the issue of publications and statements
21. To make periodic reports to stakeholders
22. To make periodic reports to relevant government ministries and departments
23. To make periodic reports to development partners where obligated
24. To issue periodic public information bulletins
25. To establish a public website
26. To establish formal links with professional associations and other bodies of stakeholders
27. To establish clear lines of authority within the MSG
28. To ensure maximum internal consultation before any statement or output is released
29. To allow members to join and leave the coalition voluntarily.

LIMITATIONS OF THE COALITION

1. Not to do anything that will inhibit or deter the participation of government and development partners in the coalition
2. Not to engage foreign experts where local ones are available
3. Not to coerce any organization into the membership of the MSG
4. Not to coerce any source of information
5. Not to accept tasks and responsibilities counter to the objectives of the MSG
6. Not to appoint or accept the formation of regional or district branches that do not have a multistakeholder outlook
7. Not to make individual pronouncements without concern to the MSG and other members
8. Not to make any commitment for the MSG without permission from the relevant unit/person vested with that authority
9. Not to bind individual members to MSG pronouncements
10. Not to undertake comparisons with other regional organizations without involving other regional multistakeholder groups
11. To discourage groupings within the coalition that are based on ethnic, political or religious philosophies
12. To focus on basic MSG objectives when seeking to join affiliations.

ETHICAL OBLIGATIONS OF MEMBERS

1. Transparency in all activities and dealings
2. Full disclosure of all financial contributions
3. Full disclosure of all technical assistance received
4. Use of data collected by the MSG for intended purposes only
5. Use of information obtained during the sessions for intended purposes only
6. Complete declaration of conflicts of interest by members.

COMMON VALUES OF MEMBERS

1. Equality in participation
2. Gender equity and sensitivity
3. Intolerance of discrimination
4. Observance of the law
5. Self-respect and self-confidence
6. Commitment to honesty
7. Mutual respect between all members of the MSG
8. Unity and focus on MSG objectives
9. Service to the public
10. Commitment to truth
11. Joint accountability
12. To be models of transparency in procurement and other day-to-day activities
13. To be models of accountability in procurement and other day-to-day activities.

Note

[1] Enepp is a dynamic, interactive web-based platform for coalition members engaged in PSM and the broader access to medicines agenda in Tanzania, Uganda and Kenya. It provides a much-needed safe zone for members to dialogue and consult around pharmaceutical PSM approaches that work, as well as discuss new ideas for catalyzing change at the country and regional level.

Client Satisfaction with Services in Uganda's Public Health Facilities: Summary of Study Findings (2013)

CLIENT SATISFACTION WITH SERVICES IN UGANDA'S PUBLIC HEALTH FACILITIES

To establish a baseline on citizen satisfaction, medicine availability, and citizen empowerment in health servicedelivery in Uganda, MeTA* conducted a survey of a broad sample of Ugandans.

47%

OVERALL SATISFACTION

(HIGH WITH PRESCRIBER...
AND LOWER WITH SERVICES)

47% is a weighted average of several percentages. For example, 71% reported being satisfied with the attitude of the prescriber, but 35% reported satisfaction with availability of laboratory services...

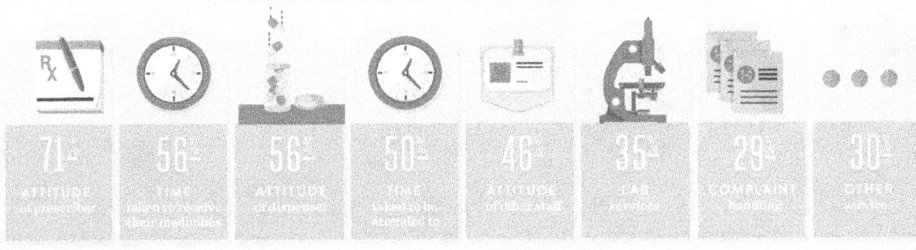

| 71% ATTITUDE of prescriber | 56% TIME taken to receive their medicines | 56% ATTITUDE of dispenser | 50% TIME taken to be attended to | 46% ATTITUDE of HF staff | 35% LAB services | 29% COMPLAINT handling | 30% OTHER service |

MORE ABOUT THE STUDY:

WHO	WHAT	WHERE	HOW	WHY
1,000'S OF UGANDANS: health facility staff, outpatients, local opinion leaders, households, community members, policy makers, and senior supply chain practitioners	RANDOM SAMPLING of data collected in 2013	10 DISTRICTS across 4 REGIONS	SURVEYS & EXIT INTERVIEWS as well as data from focus groups	SURVEYS & EXIT INTERVIEWS as well as data from focus groups

* SOURCE: Client Satisfaction with Health Services in Uganda's Public Health Facilities: A Study by the Medicines Transparency Alliance (MeTA), Uganda. December 2013. MeTA is a global alliance of governments, pharmaceutical companies, civil society, the World Health Organization, the World Bank, and other partners working to improve access to medicines by increasing accountability in the healthcare sector.

CONTACTS: Emmanuelhigenyi@gmail.com   Rkitungi@yahoo.com.

CLIENT SATISFACTION WITH SERVICES IN UGANDA'S PUBLIC HEALTH FACILITIES

To establish a baseline on citizen satisfaction, medicine availability, and citizen empowerment in health servicedelivery in Uganda, MeTA* conducted a survey of a broad sample of Ugandans.

63%

AVAILABILITY OF MEDICINES IN GENERAL

54%
AVAILABILITY
of laboratory supplies

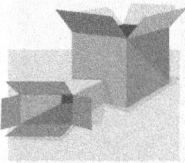

75%
AVAILABILITY
of medical sundries

70%
AVAILABILITY
of tracer medicines

68%
of PATIENTS
at all levels of facilities surveyed, received all prescribed medicines at the dispensing point

75% +
of PATIENTS
surveyed reported that they were satisfied with the availability of medicines.

MORE ABOUT THE STUDY:

WHO	WHAT	WHERE	HOW	WHY
1,000'S OF UGANDANS: health facility staff, outpatients, local opinion leaders, households, community members, policy makers, and senior supply chain practitioners	RANDOM SAMPLING of data collected in 2013	10 DISTRICTS across 4 REGIONS	SURVEYS & EXIT INTERVIEWS as well as data from focus groups	SURVEYS & EXIT INTERVIEWS as well as data from focus groups

* **SOURCE**: Client Satisfaction with Health Services in Uganda's Public Health Facilities: A Study by the Medicines Transparency Alliance (MeTA), Uganda. December 2013. MeTA is a global alliance of governments, pharmaceutical companies, civil society, the World Health Organization, the World Bank, and other partners working to improve access to medicines by increasing accountability in the healthcare sector.

CONTACTS: Emmanuelhigenyi@gmail.com   Rkitungi@yahoo.com.

CLIENT SATISFACTION WITH SERVICES IN UGANDA'S PUBLIC HEALTH FACILITIES

To establish a baseline on citizen satisfaction, medicine availability, and citizen empowerment in health servicedelivery in Uganda, MeTA* conducted a survey of a broad sample of Ugandans.

COMMUNITY OF CITIZEN ENGAGEMENT

ONLY

27%

OF SURVEY RESPONDENTS FILED A FORMAL COMPLAINT,

despite perception that people have widespread complaints about health services.

INTERESTINGLY,

49%

OF RESPONDENTS TO A FOLLOW-UP POLL REPORTED COMPLAINTS FILED.

Poll was conducted using the SMS-based U-Report platform, http://ureport.ug/.

DIFFERENCE IN FINDINGS ATTRIBUTED TO DEMOGRAPHICS.

Households on MeTA survey were rural citizens with lower levels of education; whereas U-Report respondents were self-selecting, well-educated young people with a tendency to activism.

MORE ABOUT THE STUDY:

WHO	WHAT	WHERE	HOW	WHY
1,000'S OF UGANDANS: health facility staff, outpatients, local opinion leaders, households, community members, policy makers, and senior supply chain practitioners	RANDOM SAMPLING of data collected in 2013	10 DISTRICTS across 4 REGIONS	SURVEYS & EXIT INTERVIEWS as well as data from focus groups	SURVEYS & EXIT INTERVIEWS as well as data from focus groups

* S O U R C E : Client Satisfaction with Health Services in Uganda's Public Health Facilities: A Study by the Medicines Transparency Alliance (MeTA), Uganda. December 2013. MeTA is a global alliance of governments, pharmaceutical companies, civil society, the World Health Organization, the World Bank, and other partners working to improve access to medicines by increasing accountability in the healthcare sector.

C O N T A C T S : Emmanuelhigenyi@gmail.com   Rkitungi@yahoo.com.

Bibliography

Anello, Eloy. 2008. "A Framework for Good Governance in the Public Pharmaceutical Sector." Working Draft for Field Testing and Revision, World Health Organization, Geneva.

Cabañero-Verzosa, Cecilia, and Helen R. Garcia. 2011. *People, Politics and Change: Building Communication Capacity for Reforms*. Washington, DC: World Bank.

Civil Society Profile: Tanzania. 2011. http://socs.civicus.org/CountryCivilSocietyProfiles/Tanzania.pdf.

Cohen, L., Nancy Baer, and Pam Satterwhite. 2002. "Developing Effective Coalitions: An Eight Step Guide." In *Community Health Education & Promotion: A Guide to Program Design and Evaluation*, 2nd ed., edited by M. E. Wurzbach, 144–61. Gaithersburg, MD: Aspen Publishers.

Development Partners Group Tanzania. http://www.tzdpg.or.tz/index.php?id=1164.

Draft Terms of Reference for the Pharmaceuticals Working Group (PWG) of the SWAP Committee. 2007. http://www.tzdpg.or.tz/fileadmin/documents/dpg_internal/dpg_working_groups_clusters/cluster_2/health/Sub_Sector_Group/Pharmaceuticals/TOR_SWAP_-_PHARMACEUTICALS_WG-6-6-07.pdf.

European Healthcare Fraud and Corruption Network. 2010. "The Financial Cost of Healthcare Fraud." http://www.ehfcn.org/media/documents/The-Financial-Cost-of-Healthcare-Fraud---Final-(2).pdf (accessed 2 July 2010).

Extractive Industries Transparency Initiative (EITI). 2013. http://eiti.org/eiti/requirements.

KAM Pharmaceutical & Medical Equipment Sector. 2014. http://www.kam.co.ke.

Kenya Demographic and Health Survey; Kenya National Bureau of Statistics (KNBS) 2010.

Kenya Medical Supplies Authority (KEMSA). http://kemsa.co.ke/index.php?option=com_content&view=article&id=66&Itemid=153.

Kenya Medical Supplies Authority Act 2013. http://www.kemsa.co.ke/index.php?option=com_content&view=article&id=34&Itemid (accessed June 3, 2014).

Lu, Y., et al. 2010. "Medicine Expenditures." In *The World Medicines Situation*. Geneva: World Health Organization. http://dosei.who.int/.

Management Sciences for Health. 2012. "Putting Access to Medicines at the Center of Universal Health Coverage: A Conversation with Dr. Douglas Keene." October 31. http://www.msh.org/news-events/stories/putting-access-to-medicines-at-the-center-of-universal-health-coverage-a.

Mangeni, F. 2012. "The Services Sector in Uganda. Performance in Utilisation of Trade Opportunities." http://www.ileap-jeicp.org/downloads/nairobi_nov_11/presentations/4/mangeni-service-sector-performance-ugandapptx.pdf.

MeTA (Medicines Transparency Alliance). MeTA Uganda Phase 2. http://www.medicin-estransparency.org/fileadmin/uploads/Uganda_comms_one-pager.pdf (accessed June 24).

————. 2010. *Medicines Transparency Alliance: A Review of the Pilot.* London: Medicines Transparency Alliance. http://www.medicinestransparency.org/fileadmin/uploads/Documents/MeTA_review_pilot.pdf.

Ministry of Health, Government of Uganda. 2009. "Uganda Health Sector Strategic Investment Plan (2010/11–2014/15)." http://reliefweb.int/report/uganda/uganda-health-sector-strategic-plan-iii-201011-201415.

————. 2012. "Annual Health Sector Performance Report: Financial Year 2011/12." http://reliefweb.int/sites/reliefweb.int/files/resources/Full%20Report_1045.pdf.

Namaganda, G., J. McMahan, and V. Oketcho. 2012. "Opening the Door to Understanding Staffing Needs in Uganda through the Use of WISN." http://www.intrahealth.org/blog/opening-door-understanding-staffing-needs-uganda-through-use-wisn#.U2VRM1cY33U.

Organization of Economic Cooperation and Development (OECD). See also The Kenya Health Sector Integrity Study Report 2011. http://www.tikenya.org/index.php/integrity-studies#.

Parliament of Uganda. 2013. "The Report of the Committee on Health on Ministerial Policy Statement and Budget Estimates for the Health Sector for the FY 2013/14." http://www.google.com/url?sa=t&rct=j&q=&esrc=s&source=web&cd=1&ved=0CB8QFjAA&url=http%3A%2F%2Fwww.parliament.go.ug%2Fnew%2Findex.ph.

Tanzania Demographics Profile. 2013. http://www.indexmundi.com/tanzania/demographics_profile.html.

Transparency International. 2014. http://www.transparency.org/whoweare/organisation/our_chapters.

Uganda National Health Users'/Consumers' Organisation (UNHCO) and Coalition for Health Promotion and Social Development (HEPS-Uganda). 2012. "Client Satisfaction with Health Services in Uganda: A Citizens Report Card on Selected Public Health Facilities in Bushenyi and Lira Districts." December. http://unhco.or.ug/wp-content/uploads/downloads/2013/05/CRC_UNHCO_HEPS_TAP_Final_Report_2012.pdf.

UNICEF (United Nations Children's Fund). 2012. "Cities and Children: The Challenge of Urbanisation in Tanzania." http://www.unicef.org/infobycountry/files/Cities_and_Children_-_FINAL.pdf.

United Nations. 2004. "Access to Medicines in Uganda: Intersections with Poverty: A Country Case Study." http://www.unmillenniumproject.org/documents/TF5-medicines-Appendixes.pdf.

Venture for Fund Raising. 2000. *Resource Mobilization: A Practical Guide for Research and Community Based Organizations.* 2nd ed. Ottawa: Canada International Development Research Centre.

World Bank Institute. 2013. "Improving Governance in Pharmaceutical Procurement and Supply Chain Management in Kenya, Tanzania and Uganda." http://api.ning.com/files/ZO7KDQfsD-Nzjm0vfVQTyFkZbo0sywPHwzqoQUXpnGFoDh68LhdpcP85eqvP2FrbgT3dvd0kgjH-HFuYRXgfkV*q50MxQttI/PSMinAfricacountries_24June.pdf (accessed on April 24, 2014).

———. 2013. "Monitoring Pharmaceutical Procurement and Stock Levels of Selected Essential Medicines in Dodoma: A Pilot by the Multi-stakeholder Group in Pharmaceutical Procurement in Tanzania."

World Health Organization (WHO). 2011. "The World Medicines Situation 2011: Good Governance for the Pharmaceutical Sector." World Health Organization, Geneva. http://apps.who.int/medicinedocs/documents/s18061en/s18061en.pdf (accessed April 14, 2014).

———. 2013. http://www.who.int/mediacentre/factsheets/fs355/en/.

———. 2014. "United Republic of Tanzania: Health Profile." http://www.who.int/gho/countries/tza.pdf.

WHO Regional Office for Africa. 2009. "WHO Country Cooperation Strategy 2010–2015." Tanzania.

Environmental Benefits Statement

The World Bank is committed to reducing its environmental footprint. In support of this commitment, the Publishing and Knowledge Division leverages electronic publishing options and print-on-demand technology, which is located in regional hubs worldwide. Together, these initiatives enable print runs to be lowered and shipping distances decreased, resulting in reduced paper consumption, chemical use, greenhouse gas emissions, and waste.

The Publishing and Knowledge Division follows the recommended standards for paper use set by the Green Press Initiative. Whenever possible, books are printed on 50 percent to 100 percent postconsumer recycled paper, and at least 50 percent of the fiber in our book paper is either unbleached or bleached using Totally Chlorine Free (TCF), Processed Chlorine Free (PCF), or Enhanced Elemental Chlorine Free (EECF) processes.

More information about the Bank's environmental philosophy can be found at http://crinfo.worldbank.org/wbcrinfo/node/4.

green
press
INITIATIVE